TIME *to* GRIEVE

365 Steps to Self-Confidence

A programme for personal transformation in just a few minutes a day

'... follow the 52 themed chapters, including exercises, insights
and practical hints on how to overcome your lack of self-esteem
and begin to live life to the full now, not tomorrow!' – *Good Health*

Learning to Counsel

Develop the skills you need to counsel others

'A counsellor's pocketbook and a useful companion to students on courses up
to counselling certificate level.' – *Counselling and Psychotherapy Journal*

Death and Probate

A self-help guide to managing the procedures yourself

'The author is obviously a master of his subject.' – Amazon reader review

howtobooks

Send for a free copy of the latest catalogue to:

How To Books
3 Newtec Place, Magdalen Road,
Oxford OX4 1RE, United Kingdom
email: info@howtobooks.co.uk
http://www.howtobooks.co.uk

TIME *to* GRIEVE

HOW TO COME THROUGH BEREAVEMENT TO RECOVERY AND GROWTH

2nd EDITION

Michael Dunn

howtobooks

First published by How To Books Ltd,
3 Newtec Place, Magdalen Road,
Oxford OX4 1RE, United Kingdom
Tel: 01865 798306 Fax: 01865 248780
info@howtobooks.co.uk
www.howtobooks.co.uk

First published 2000
Second edition 2006

British Library Cataloguing in Publication Data
A catalogue record for this book is available from
the British Library

Cover design by Baseline Arts, Oxford
Produced for How To Books by Deer Park Productions,
Tavistock
Typeset by PDQ Typesetting, Stoke-on-Trent, Staffs.
Printed and bound in Great Britain by Cromwell Press Ltd,
Trowbridge, Wiltshire

Note: The material contained in this book is set out in good
faith for general guidance and no liability can be accepted for
loss or expenses incurred as a result of relying in particular
circumstances on statements made in the book. The laws and
regulations are complex and liable to change, and readers
should check the current position with the relevant
authorities before making personal arrangements.

Contents

Preface

It all starts with love.

Love between partners, friends, neighbours, colleagues; men and women, same-sex love; creative, spiritual love as well as the manipulative, abusive sort; love in its broad, comfortable everyday sense but, also, at its fiercest and most obsessive.

Every time we allow someone into our lives we invest part of ourselves in the relationship. The personal gains we make – companionship, sharing resources, emotional support, creating a family – are offset by the compromises we make – dependence, emotional commitment, responsibilities 'in sickness and in health'.

Our engagement in relationships can be slight and casual or lifelong and total. By the time a 50-year-long partnership has passed we may well have forgotten *where* and *when* we invested *what* parts of ourselves in it: our separate identities have become fused into one.

When someone dies in a close relationship, the survivor can be left stranded and alone with an identity requiring two people to be viable.

In order to recover our stability we need to dismantle the reliance and expectations we have had on this joint identity: we need to unpick the commitments we gave to it – recover our emotional deposits and investments. We need to rebuild something that resembles our old individuality using what psychological, emotional and practical materials we can find on the site of the disaster. We need to re-trace our steps – at a time when we may never have had less strength or interest.

As someone famously said *'It's like falling in love backwards.'*

We tend to regard bereavement as an inevitable catastrophe that hits us after the death of a loved one: the greater the love the harder we're hit. Those around us expect – sometimes to the point of insistence – that we submit ourselves to a black despair: tears are expected and comfort should be welcomed.

We tend to have a clear notion of the concepts of 'taking it well' and 'taking it badly' and we will make quiet judgements about the reactions of grieving people.

It may be that most of us are so unfamiliar with death that we have this simple idea of grief. In reality, the way that we react to a death will be intensely personal. Our response will depend upon:

◆ the impact the dead person had on our lives,
◆ what personal psychological resources we have developed
◆ how we have learned to deal with loss earlier in our lives.

Because these three factors will vary widely between us, so will the quality and extent of our grief. All bereavements are different and where we come on the scale of 'no grief' to 'devastation' should be respected and supported.

Grief has come to have apparently different meanings according to where we stand. Different people will consider it:

◆ a social ritual   ◆ a psychiatric illness
◆ a straightforward sadness ◆ a family crisis
◆ a religious duty   ◆ post-traumatic stress
◆ something to be avoided   ◆ a total tragedy.

It seems to me unhelpful to see grief from any *one* of these perspectives. I have tried to focus on the subject as a basic human experience: the emotional, psychological, physical and social response to the loss of someone close.

I have also tried to be positive about the subject. Much writing about bereavement is gloomy, dramatically emotional and solemn, emphasising pain and 'unusual', destructive – almost shameful – behaviour.

Grief is inevitably painful, but it is normal and natural. It can cause problems and we may need specialised help. However, mostly, bereavement is something we can anticipate and pass through. It can also be a positive time when families and communities can re-affirm relationships, when the future can be re-assessed and when new directions can be explored.

Far from being a shameful, unfortunate, furtive and morbid affair, dying and bereavement are natural parts of life and relationships. We need to acknowledge the painfulness and potential damage of the process. However we also need to find the courage to acknowledge the opportunities for regeneration, change and personal growth.

Grief, of course, is not only a part of profound human relationships: it can follow the loss of anyone or anything where we have made an attachment. We can even feel genuine grief and tears on the death of a TV soap character with whom we have 'lived' for many years.

Later on we'll look at some particular types of grief but mostly I have found myself returning to examples of grief involving people in long-term partner-relationships.

Michael Dunn

CHAPTER 1

The Causes of Grief

W e can be forgiven for thinking that the reason people grieve is straightforward. When we lose someone we love we need time to adjust to life without them – grief is the hurt we have to endure during this process. However, because grief can be such a significant part of life, there has been no shortage of theories about its cause and how to deal with it.

Some explanations

It's an illness...

Grief is painful and is often described in terms of physical symptoms – indeed there *are* often signs of ill health. There is also, in time, a natural 'recovery'. The temptation to think of it as a disease is dangerous because the implication is that we are helpless and will only 'get well' with help from outside. We may not feel encouraged to look to our own inner resources (which ultimately are our only key to 'recovery').

It's a physical thing...

This is the view that bereavement represents a shutting down of activity following the trauma of a death. The body needs time and space to reorganise and begin to construct a new way of living. Because all our energy is focused on this shock absorption and reconstruction process, our respiratory, circulatory, nutritional and immune systems may suffer reduced efficiency. This emphasises the need to look after ourselves while we grieve.

As Freud said...

The traditional psychiatric explanation of grief is that when we lose an important relationship we need to take possession of the dead person's identity and, step by step, to unhook all the ties that bound us to them. In this way we can eventually be free to put our living relationship with them to rest and be able to resume a normal life.

Problems will arise if these ties have been eroded by mixed feelings or guilt: we might not have the strength to release them on our own and we may need some outside help – not necessarily psychiatric help but another perspective to tease out the reality of our thoughts and feelings.

Whilst this may be a useful way of looking at the complexities of bereavement, our everyday experience of loss may become confused and difficult to deal with if we start to be too analytical.

It's all in the mind ...

This comes from the idea that the reality of our lives, and how we regard the world, is constructed in our own minds as a result of our past experiences. We constantly measure what is happening now in relation to what happened in the past. In this way we can predict future behaviour and feelings. The more rigid expectations are, the more hurt we shall be when we lose a major component – such as a partner. The work of grieving involves reconstructing our world model so that it 'works' without the dead person. The general lesson this teaches us is to take nothing for granted, not to make assumptions and to expect the unexpected.

Everything has an evolutionary purpose ...

Grief can be seen as behaviour designed to express pain and helplessness to other people and to look to them for support. In this way we can all look after each other in times of distress.

Different cultures and religions all give priority to bereaved people. The rituals surrounding funerals and dealing with mourning all contribute to a reaffirmation of the society's beliefs and the healing of the scar in the family or group caused by the death.

These are all interesting and valid ways of regarding bereavement. For our purposes, however, I would like to concentrate on grief as being caused by the *loss of an attachment to someone.*

A working hypothesis

> *He didn't take all I had, I didn't give it to him outright . . . it*
> *was a loan. It's time for me to take it back again now.*
>
> Widow, aged 55 years

We are brought up to think of 'love' as a romantic, spiritual state tinged with 'magic' and 'decreed by fate'. It's as though love was something 'other' and independent which 'happens' to us whether we like it or not: we don't plan or prepare to love someone – we 'fall'.

We like this idea because it ties us into a relationship in a way that seems to transcend day-to-day life: we suddenly feel 'better' than we really are – the 'cloud-nine' feeling.

It's also very convenient socially, emotionally, economically and biologically to be in a love relationship. There are some big pay-offs.

◆ We can develop a closeness to someone, which is comforting and supportive.
◆ We can share responsibilities for living: there's too much to do in life for one person to manage everything properly.
◆ We can share our incomes – two can live as cheaply as one.
◆ We can finish with the demanding business of 'finding' a boyfriend or girlfriend and get down to more important things in life.
◆ For most people, they now have the optimum conditions for the biggest pay-off – making babies.

When things go right we will both 'play the game' and work together to look after our new-found love for each other. It won't be easy – it needs:

◆ commitment
◆ sensitivity
◆ fidelity
◆ responsibility
◆ planning and budgeting
◆ skills of parenthood (eventually).

If we can manage it, this is a wonderful system for living a fulfilled and rewarding life in all respects – emotional, sexual, social, psychological, economical. The alternative life of serial (often shallow) relationships with its self-sufficiency, loneliness, emotional and sexual dissatisfactions, is a miserable one.

What we don't always realise is that the 'love' that underpins such relationships is *not* magical. It's driven by mutual self-interest and primitive urges to promote the succession of our genes through our children. In many ways 'love' is a harmless metaphor – why shouldn't we clothe genetic competition in something more acceptable which gives pleasure to all. To be continuously preoccupied with our crude, basic urges would be depressing and tedious. 'Love' is a good idea.

> *Their lives had intertwined into a comfortable dependency,*
> *like the gnarled wisteria on their front porch, still twisted*
> *around the frail support which long ago it had outgrown.*
> Don Wolf, *The Night of the Falling Stone*, 1963

Mostly, if we are in a settled, fulfilling long-term relationship we dwell on our good fortune and look forward to the good times ahead. This is much more fun than looking at the dangers involved. However, we are so interested in enjoying the positive sides to the relationship that we pay little attention to the compromises that we make to maintain it:

◆ When we give a long-term commitment to someone we are choosing to put most of our emotional eggs in one basket.

◆ When we are sensitive to each other's feelings we tune in to their particular wavelength and develop an awareness of moods and body language that is special exclusively to them.

◆ We usually develop complementary roles in our life together which is a useful way of organising things – but it *does* mean that we may give away certain skills – money management, cookery, gardening, etc. – to our partner.

◆ As parents, traditional 'mother' and 'father' roles may have led women to become caring and communicative and men to become 'strong', with a sharper focus away from the home. (These roles, of course, are in the process of radical change.)

◆ Our 'faithfulness' and loyalty causes us, over time, to lose our interest and aptitude for developing other 'big' relationships.

These compromises can work like clockwork for a lifetime in the whole family's interest. The trouble starts when one of the people in such a mutually dependent, locked-in relationship dies. The above compromises – and others that only *we* know about – come home to roost.

- ◆ We have become used to the intimacy and richness of a relationship that is special and irreplaceable. We are threatened with forthcoming isolation and loneliness.
- ◆ We may have always depended on the dead person to give us emotional support when we were troubled in the past. Ironically, at this time of our greatest need they're not there. Moreover, we don't know how to be easily comforted by 'strangers'. Bereavement in these circumstances can be like releasing a zoo-bred animal into the wild.
- ◆ To make life easy, we gave away whole parts of our life and now our delegated skills and knowledge have died with our partner.
- ◆ Our whole way of life, after so many years, has been turned upside down: we may be completely at a loss to know what to do or say. We'll certainly be fearful about the prospect of the further changes to come.
- ◆ There may be a strong impulse to restore the *status quo* but we haven't the strength, energy, skill or knowledge to do it.

This is loss. The repair work that we have to do is grief.

Although loss is most evident following successful life partnerships – we can find it in all aspects of our life: work, possessions, abilities, illness, money, pets. Wherever we invite something or somebody into our lives and give them a special importance – the greater our loss will be when they go. We created the situation, we took the risk, we gave them responsibility for parts of our lives. We might have been wise or foolish to do it, they may, or may not, have deserved our attention – it doesn't matter: we're left with exactly the same substance – grief.

How much or how little grief is up to us to decide, governed by how much we were attached. The grief that we feel for TV celebrities, pets, jobs, marriages, sentimentally valued ornaments has been 'our business' and the way that their loss affects us will be special to the investment we put into them.

The theft of a dead mother's wedding ring (with the symbolism attached) may have a greater impact on someone than the death of a relative. This means:

◆ We should be free to acknowledge that apparently small losses can have big impacts.

◆ We should put more dramatic losses into perspective. The causes and effects may be huge but it's never 'the end of the world'. We are not 'tragic victims' – we will usually be able to find our own way of repairing our lives, particularly if we have some good friends.

What happens after we die?

Most of our feelings following a death will be connected with our sense of loss. However, they will be coloured greatly by our previously held beliefs about the meaning of death.

The problem for most of us is that the subject of death is so shrouded in fearfulness and taboo that we usually have only a half-formed, vague idea of what happens to us after we die.

Nevertheless, we'll usually have some idea in our minds about what death is. We may have received these ideas unconsciously in childhood, they may be cultural or religious teachings, they may have been formed by our experience or personality or we may have given the subject some logical attention.

◆ 'Death is an improved state of being. A condition without human frailty, hostility or materialistic values.' (We can have our own regrets but, at least, the dead person has moved on to a better life. This can be a great consolation.)

◆ 'Death means Judgement Day. An all-knowing God will analyse the way we have lived our lives and decide whether we are worthy to move to better things or be punished eternally.' (This will make death hard to accept. We all know how hard it is to measure up to absolute standards and how vulnerable we all would be to this sort of evaluation. It might be worse if the death was sudden – if the dead person had no time to 'repent' and 'make their peace'.)

◆ 'Death is an opportunity for rebirth: a second chance to get things right.' (This is an optimistic outlook: there has been no absolute loss – the dead person has simply moved on to greater opportunities. We can even be pleased for them – all we have to worry about is our own sense of loss. It's not so far-fetched – the philosopher Voltaire wrote: 'After all, it is no more surprising to be born twice than it is to be born once.')

◆ 'Death is nothingness: a biological event. We cease to exist in any form at all.' (This removes any anxieties about the dead person's fate in the future but it focuses attention on regrets about the fullness of their life and how we contributed to it.)

We may have heard of 'near death experiences'. These are reported accounts by people who have been on the very edge of death who have recovered. They have very similar features:

◆ there is a feeling of hope, peace and well-being
◆ there is no fear or pain
◆ on their 'return' people are much more settled and they lose anxieties about death.

In spite of the logical explanation that these experiences are simply a result of hallucination caused by a failing oxygen supply, these reports remain intriguing and not fully explained. Whatever the experience is about, it does give some encouragement even to non-religious people to think that death may not be the gloomy tragedy we believed. This can soften the grief of survivors.

There are many ways in which we can make sense of death in this way and, whichever we choose, it will remain in the background to our loss, supporting our recovery or intensifying our pain.

Death isn't strictly the end . . .

No friendship dieth
With death of any day,
No true friendship lieth
Cold with lifeless clay.
Though our boyhood's playtime
Be gone with summer's breath
No friendship fades with Maytime
No friendship dies with death.

Epitaph to J.R.S., Compton, Surrey

A common feature of most world religions is the concept of death not being the end: our present life is seen as a preparation for the hereafter. There is tremendous comfort to many people in the prospect of being reunited with loved ones – the loss is softened.

People who are not adherents to religion feel the same need to find reasons for immortality:

◆ We live on in the memories of other people.

◆ Our genes are physically transmitted to the next generation.

◆ Our physical bodies revert to nutrients for plant growth.

If we wish to see the death of a loved one not as final, but as part of a continuum, we may gain much comfort but we should not blind ourselves to the present – and continuing – reality of their absence.

The temptation of believing that a dead person continues to live on another level is seductive but if that means we spend years trying to contact their 'spirit' we are distracting ourselves from facing up to the reality of our own grief for their loss.

It's probably best to stick to the comforting metaphor of poetry:

Do not stand at my grave and weep -
I am not there, I do not sleep.
I am a thousand winds that blow;
I am the diamond glints on snow.
I am the sunlight on ripened grain;
I am the gentle autumn's rain.
When you awaken in the morning's hush,
I am the swift uplifting rush
Of quiet birds in circled flight,
I am the soft star that shines at night.
Do not stand at my grave and cry,
I am not there; I did not die.

Mahkah Native Indian Prayer

Grieving is only
love in another
key.
LAWRENCE
WHISTLER

CHAPTER 2

The Process of Grieving

Whilst it isn't helpful to describe a series of stages of bereavement – as though each was a graduation from the previous one – there *are* characteristic responses which tend to follow severe loss. These are ways of coping with the unmanageable and gradually settling into 'useful' grieving.

'There's been a mistake – she went to Manchester today.'

It is not so much that we irrationally deny that a death has occurred – it is more that, for a while, we cannot conceive the world without the person we have lost. Smaller losses in life are no problem – our own experience and imagination will enable us to take them in our stride. However, if we have become very dependent on the person who has died, we are suddenly left apparently with no support and unable to continue. Before we can take the time to understand the reality, we are forced into some reaction: if we are not to collapse completely our only other choice is to resort to the temporary – but protective – first-aid of denial.

'Of course I'm bloody angry; wouldn't you be?'

I felt like a tree, split by lightning – roots exposed.

Mary Jones

As we emerge from the anaesthesia of denial, the rawness of our hurt can show in a fearful search for explanation of the death. Something or somebody must be to blame for this catastrophe: 'there is a reason for everything'.

We have three choices for 'blame' (four if we find a belief in God is shaken).

◆ The doctor, the hospital, the wrong treatment, the drunken driver, the murderer, the railway company, 'society'. This is the easiest choice: someone out there had caused the death and our hurt. It can feel good to be able to direct our feelings against someone who may or may not have been directly responsible. We can consider ourselves 'victims' which may, at least, be a role with which we are familiar.

◆ We may (or may not) have good reason to believe that the dead person was responsible for their own death. Maybe they were the drunk driver. 'If only he'd gone to the doctor last year'; 'Nobody needs to go rock-climbing'; 'What about us who are left to pick up the pieces?'

This is dangerous ground. It is hard to hold the positive memories and sense of loss alongside feelings of resentment and fury: they each interfere with our ability to focus on the other. Our ambivalence confuses us – we may be drawn into saying things which perhaps ought to remain not only unsaid, but unthought.

◆ We may search our imagination to find some word or action of our own that may conceivably have changed the way things turned out. It seems the most straightforward and least provocative way of looking for responsibility but, unfortunately, it is also the most self-destructive.

We almost always overestimate our own responsibility for events but once the fantasy becomes embedded in our sorrow it will gnaw away and become an unreasonable reality to us. Without people around us to give reassurance, it can, in extreme situations, stay with us for the rest of our lives.

The truth is, of course, that we rarely have any responsibility for someone's death. Even death through accident or negligence is not intended. However, in our hunger for making sense of catastrophe we'll try to personalise it. And we're hardest on ourselves.

An exception is suicide, which often happens within difficult relationships: we might have made a difference there – but more about that on page 111.

Anger seems such a senseless, inappropriate feeling to have about someone who has died – who could possibly be blamed for dying? Grown-ups know how silly and unreasonable it is – and yet this sharp, resentful feeling can persist: it seems so childish.

In fact this apparently inexplicable feeling *can* so often be rooted in our early childhood. When a young child is separated from its parent for an appreciable time its first response when reunited is not overwhelming relief and pleasure, but furious anger. It has been suggested that this 'disciplining' of the errant parent is genetically programmed into our infancy to make sure our parent thinks twice about re-offending: babies know how vital parental access is and sometimes they need to emphasise it if there is 'parental carelessness'.

When we are bereaved in adulthood we are vulnerable and our first responses to major loss are those last used when we were toddlers – even though we know they are unreasonable and illogical.

'He just sits there, doctor: staring at the lawn.'

> *Grief makes one hour ten.*
>
> Shakespeare, *Richard II*

Usually in life, as we get older, we learn how to solve problems. We may not be successful but, mostly, we know all about complaining, negotiating, repairing marriages and calling emergency plumbers. Some problems are enormous and are beyond our resources – but at least we know that, if we chose to, we could achieve almost anything we want.

The loss of a loved one, however, may be the first time in adulthood that we are faced with something to which there seems no solution. The last time we felt like this was when we were three and became separated from our mother in the market – utterly at a loss about what to do. When we were three we were soon re-united and within 20 minutes everything returned to normal. Now, as an adult we can relive that toddler panic – but without any further prospect of seeing our 'mother' ever again. We *will* regain our survival skills – but not yet for a while.

Apart from the hurt of it all, our self-esteem may be dented if we are normally someone who is used to being on top of things. We may be hit with the realisation that ultimately we are without the power we thought we had: some things can't be fixed – the most important things. This is just a short thought away from the sober truth of the inevitability of our *own* death: we knew, in principle, that one day we might die, but we would see what we could do about that when the time came.

'I just don't seem to be able to settle to anything.'

With some people there's also an irrational, restless yearning – a need to search for the dead person. It is as though, in spite of our brain knowing the reality, our muscles are helplessly programmed not to leave any stone unturned. There is some comfort in long walks around places familiar to the person in life and unconscious scanning of faces in crowds sometimes has mistaken results. A variation of this restlessness can show itself in compulsive behaviour: the sort of manic activity which can make others – and us – think that we may be losing our minds:

◆ the three-hour washing and ironing session at 4am
◆ the daily jog to the point of exhaustion
◆ the complete spring-clean that *'must be done'* by the time of the funeral.

Although such obsessional behaviour appears bizarre and worrying, it is not necessarily a sign of breakdown. There is some satisfaction to be gained: it is a way of channelling massive reserves of energy constructively. In the midst of our vulnerability and helplessness we can, at least, do something where we have *some* control.

Sometimes we can be surprised (and ashamed) by a marked feeling of euphoria. However, this has nothing to do with happiness but is a purely physical side effect of hormone changes in reaction to shock. It's only the sort of 'high' we get after intense exercise but it can give us a deceptive feeling of spirituality and sharp sensitivity.

'And then he just snapped at me, "Why don't you go home now...."'

It's easy to take offence at the slightest thing: 'insensitive nosiness'; 'stupid questions'; 'questionable motives'.

Funeral directors are often unfortunate targets: they have no previous relationship with the family, they're being paid well to deal with the funeral and there is an enormous potential for them to get things 'not quite right'.

◆ 'I can't stand his artificial solemnity.'
◆ 'She had a very casual manner.'
◆ 'He was wearing *brown* shoes.'

Such barbed, unreasonable anger can be hurtful but it does serve to give us a small opportunity of taking a grip on life when we are feeling otherwise disorientated.

> *Rage creeps up on you unawares. I was coming back from London and as I walked along a crowded compartment and saw people laughing and talking and reading and sleeping, something in my mind went briefly out of gear. Their normality was hideous to me. I was in hostile country, an enemy alien.*
>
> Mary Stott, *The Guardian*

It's as though such 'thoughtless' behaviour was deliberately insulting – 'How can they be so casual and disrespectful; they must know he died two days ago.'

At other times this anger may simply be the outward expression of our own inability to cope.

> *Remember, anger is almost the first response to anything, however kindly meant.*
>
> Virginia Ironside, *You'll Get Over It!*, 1996

'She broke down and wept – even though she was only a distant cousin...'

Often a bereavement can trigger connections with previous losses. It's as though the present shock activates and opens our mental cupboard of unresolved grief and this undone work from the past becomes attached to our present bereavement. Also, the way we are feeling now may remind us of past pain.

This may explain why we often experience the keenest grief for people with whom we had the most difficult relationships.

People who have had open, shared and mature relationships are much less likely to be burdened with regrets and unfinished business: they can simply concentrate on the sadness of the present time and then to look to the future.

'And he was standing there as plain as you ...'

> *The dead are often just as living as the living are, only we cannot get them to believe it. They can come to us but, till we die, we cannot go to them. To be dead is to be able to understand that one is alive.*
>
> Samuel Butler (1835–1902), *Notebooks*

With so much energy invested in the searching, it is not surprising that many people 'find' the person who has died. In one study (W. D. Rees *British Medical Journal,* 1967) found that 39 per cent of 293 bereaved spouses had experienced a sense of the presence of their partner: 14 per cent had actually had hallucinations or illusions of a physical presence. Generally these were people who were older, lonelier and more bereft than others – but their experiences, far from making things worse, seemed to have a positive, helpful effect. In any case, there is enough evidence to show that such sensations can be a normal part of bereavement and not an indication of psychiatric illness.

Similarly about 50 per cent of people take their grief to bed with them and report the presence of the dead person in dreams. These usually evoke happy memories – only to be shattered in the cold light of day.

'She grows more like him every day ...'

Another way in which survivors cling on to the memory of the person they have lost is to develop symptoms similar to those leading up to the death. Similarly, we might adopt habits, interests and mannerisms which characterised the dead person:

> *A hitherto rather dull wife whose witty husband had died surprised herself and all around her by her newly acquired gift of repartee. She tried to explain this by saying alternately, 'I have to do it for him now' or, 'It isn't really me, he speaks out of me' (like a ventriloquist).*
>
> Lily Pincus, *Death in the Family,* 1976

'He's just been dead six weeks and I can't remember what he looks like...'

> For various reasons... my heart was lighter than it had been for many weeks. For one thing, I suppose I am recovering physically from a good deal of mere exhaustion... And suddenly at the very moment when, so far, I mourned H. least, I remembered her best...
>
> Why has no one told me these things? How easily I might have misjudged another man in the same situation? I might have said, 'He's got over it. He's forgotten his wife,' when the truth was, 'He remembers her better because he's partly got over it.'
>
> C. S. Lewis (1898–1963), *A Grief Observed*

It seems puzzling that partners can have been together for many years and yet can, so soon, go out of focus for their survivor. It could simply be an unconscious way of avoiding the pain of the loss – we block out memories, which fuel the hurt. More commonly, however, this lack of clarity comes after a long, close relationship. We have been so linked to a partner in so many complex ways, that, so near to their loss, we have difficulty in keeping them in our mind as a whole. The very act of deliberately straining to hold on to their presence in our mind makes things harder. It may be only later, when we have cleared away some of the confusion, that we can really grasp the full reality of our memories. C. S. Lewis described this very well some months after his wife died.

> ...as I have discovered, passionate grief does not link us with the dead but cuts us off from them. This becomes clearer and clearer. It is just at those moments when I feel least sorrow – getting into my morning bath is one of them – that H. rushes upon my mind in her full reality, her otherness. Not, as in my worst moments, all fore-shortened and patheticised and solemnized by miseries, but as she is in her own right. This is good and tonic.
>
> C. S. Lewis (1898–1963), *A Grief Observed*

'*I keep going over those last few days in my mind...*'

Normally when we are faced with significant problems in our lives we like to have full information and a chance to influence what the effect on us will be.

When someone close dies unexpectedly or after a very short illness we are cheated of this involvement. Often this has been such a disaster for us that we sometimes can't resist the temptation to replay the time leading to the death: we meticulously examine how our intervention could have made a difference.

Because it is a fantasy (and we know it) we shall always be frustrated by the reality of their death without our involvement: this might lead us to start the process all over again ... and again.

Although this may seem an unhealthy obsession at the time it does have a positive aspect. By pretending things had been otherwise – 'If only I'd insisted on driving' – we imaginatively become engaged in the drama leading to the death: there is a greater sense of completeness.

We can also imagine important final conversations – what were the words we both left unsaid?

'*She seems much more settled in herself...*'

The dramatic time of acute shock and sharp distress comes to a close. It is now time for the quieter, more long-lived phases of bereavement to set in.

When we live in a continuing relationship our native optimism gives us a continuing (maybe unrealistic) hope that, together we can sort out any difficulties between us.

The moment someone close to us dies, however, the state of our relationship becomes frozen. What we are left with will be with us forever. We are left with an emotional snapshot of how things were at the time of the death.

When we suffer normally – from an illness perhaps – we are sustained by the thought that we will get better and we can look forward to noticeable improvements. The quality of grief suffering, however, is different. For a time we don't want things to get better – fresh grief involves a yearning to go backwards, not forwards.

A friend assured me in his letter that though I could not see beyond the suffering, I should in time come through it. I laughed that his consolation should be so unconsoling; for I wanted nothing better than to live always in the immediacy of the loss. In the sharpness of it I felt near to her. The worst was the best.

Lawrence Whistler, *The Initials in the Heart*, 1987

If the memory of the dead person is fixed at a time when there were unresolved difficulties, we are left stranded and impotent with a situation, which we shall never again be able to influence.

'I just feel so "down" all the time...'

We are used to being in an active relationship where hurts can be repaired: where there is always room for improvement. Our inability to have any further effect on things – at the very moment when we have been deprived of our main support – can paralyse us emotionally and this helplessness can easily slide into depression.

It is cruel that this will also be happening at a time when other pressures begin to make demands. Following the death there may be threats of money problems, difficulties with housing or family relationships; we may, ourselves, need to give support to other dependants. Within days we will be called on to make a formal public appearance at the funeral – the centre of attention – and then, to some extent, to act as host to the funeral gathering.

At best we will have been well prepared for the death, have had a good relationship, a large family, supportive friends and no financial worries. At worst we will be young, with children, little support, few resources and the death will have been unexpectedly sudden.

We should be concerned if we were *not* depressed in such circumstances. We should expect that for some days, weeks or months there will be a muddled change in our feelings and behaviour. However, if there is an *increase* or *persistence* in some of the symptoms of depression we should take notice. Some of these symptoms are:

- ◆ sleep disturbance
- ◆ low energy
- ◆ loss of concentration
- ◆ confused thinking
- ◆ obsessive behaviour.

- ◆ tearfulness
- ◆ loss of appetite
- ◆ anxiety
- ◆ poor memory

If we are alone the despair – if unsupported – may not be interrupted: there may be no one to nudge us into different ways of thinking and feeling. Also isolation gives us less motivation to keep up with our daily routine, standards of housekeeping, personal appearance and social behaviour.

These can all be signs of a normal response to the loss of someone close: we shouldn't think that we are suffering from some disorder. Our GP may offer us a short-term course of anti-depressants. She is not trying to fob us off with tablets – modern anti-depressants can be dramatically effective in giving a lift that gives us the confidence and strength to cope. Usually our need for such a welcome chemical crutch is short-lived and we shouldn't be surprised if the doctor is reluctant to continue the prescription – the grief work to come is best done with a clear head.

'She's coping very well in the circumstances.'

Many people become very skilful at preventing grief intruding into consciousness. These are people who believe themselves to be in charge of feelings and experiences from their past. Maturity will tell us the truth, however – they are normally in charge of us. Just as stress involves pent-up undischarged energy, grief involves unexpressed and often confused feelings of loss, desertion, anger, guilt, love, fear, helplessness – we'll have our own list.

There is something almost tangible about these feelings. It is as though there were a measurable amount of 'grief-stuff' stored in the body under pressure. We won't be 'better' until we are rid of it.

We can discharge it quickly, in liquefied form, through our tear ducts, we can form it as accurately as possible into spoken or written words or we can seal it up and not allow ourselves or anybody else to get near it.

The trouble is we can never really contain it: it generally finds a way out. It might explode painfully under the mounting pressure in ten years time or, more likely, its harmful influence will seep, a few molecules a day, into all parts of the body appearing as anxiety, depression, insomnia and all sorts of aches and pains: this could last up to a lifetime.

On the other hand, there are some people who have developed the trick of coping with difficult feelings by simply setting them aside and refusing – successfully – to deal with them. We may be shocked and anxious to 'help him to get in touch with his feelings' but we ought to be cautious about such ruthless invasion of someone's defence mechanisms – it may cause more harm than good.

'Now that he's dead I can start to go to the cinema again.'

As we come through the turbulence of the shock we look around us and begin to take stock of our new situation: we compare our life now to what it was before the death. For some people who have experienced the sudden death of a loved one there will be a yearning to put the clock back. For others, however, the death will have been the climax of months of anxiety, distress and physical and emotional caring.

It would be unsurprising if part of us was not immensely *relieved* at the lifting of this emotional and physical burden. However, our first response to this sense of relief may be guilt: it can seem shocking to look forward to our own comfort after someone's death. It's hard to remember that we are very complicated people with many strands to our lives and many mixed feelings. Simultaneously we would do anything for the death not to have happened *and* we are pleased that we can resume other aspects or our lives. These facts are *both* true but they are *not* connected.

Often, if the end has been hard and painful, we will be pleased that the dead person is no longer suffering. It is perfectly normal and acceptable for us also to feel some respite. It is one of the first signs of strength for the recovery to come.

'I keep taking one step forward and two steps back...'

She said it was like a minefield – you never knew when you were going to stumble on a tripwire.

Bet Wiseman

Our previous experience of ordinary pain is that it begins severely and gradually reduces at a regular rate until we recover. Most people who are bereaved are surprised that grief doesn't seem to work like that.

... it is more accurate to describe the process like a roller coaster of many ups and downs with gradual improvement over time... The early months following the loss were the most difficult and these early indicators were relatively good predictors of long-term adjustment. The ups and downs of the roller coaster can easily be precipitated by mistakenly seeing the face of the deceased in a crowd, hearing an old familiar song on the radio, driving by the hospital where the spouse was treated, or conversely, feeling proud for successfully balancing a chequebook for the first time, meeting a new friend at a club, or simply mastering the timer of a microwave oven.

Lund, 1989 (reported in *The Handbook of Grief,* 1993

The body has a system for dealing with pain – it won't allow us to experience more than we can stand: when it gets too much it will switch off. People suffering the agony of burns report that there are occasional moments of numbness when the pain will subside. The same applies to emotional pain. Our minds seem to have safety valves, which can shut down distress when it threatens to overwhelm us. It's worth keeping this in mind – a breathing space is just around the corner.

The sense of loss wells up, a feeling so intense that one cannot imagine an end to it. But then, after a time, the numbness comes, a period of calm and relief. Soon numbness is replaced by another wave of loss. And so it continues: waves of loss, calmness, loss, calmness. This is the natural cycle of pain. And as soon as you reach an overload, your emotions shut off, you literally stop feeling for a little while. These waves continue with smaller amplitudes and longer rest periods, until the hurt finally ceases.

Matthew Kay and Patrick Fleming, *Self Esteem,* 1987

'It makes you think...'

Death is a crisis that forces all concerned – the dying and their bereaved survivors – to look at the 'meaning' of their lives. In between births and deaths we are easily distracted by the business of living, but when we are faced with our own imminent death or the loss of an important relationship, we cannot avoid taking stock of what we have been doing with our lives. We need to evaluate our existence.

In a close relationship where we have lost someone, a large part of our life may have been dismantled and we are going to have to work out how to keep things going until we can rebuild things. Whatever happens, we are not going to be able to continue as before.

There are two extreme ways of proceeding.

◆ If we have had an open, 'mature' and 'honest' relationship, which preserved our independence, it will not be too difficult to adjust. The hooks of dependence will have been only lightly attached and we can recover easily those parts of ourselves which we had invested in the relationship.

◆ We can shut off those parts of ourselves where we used to be closely dependent on the dead person. We may be so lacking in inner resources or outside support (or both) that we take on a new role as a disabled 'victim'. Some people can retain this disability for the rest of their lives.

The biological purpose of grief

Sorrow that has no vent in tears makes other organs weep.

Anon.

People report feeling better after a cry, according to a study by University of Minnesota biochemist, William Frey who discovered the neurotransmitters leucine and prolactin in emotional tears; the substances were not found in tears shed in response to sliced onions. Tears may help the body alleviate stress and cleanse itself of toxins, as do other exocrine processes, e.g. sweat, urine, and exhaled air.

Women cry five times more frequently than men. Women's tears also flow down the face more than men's – where they

*well up in the eye. The average length of a crying spell is one
to two minutes.'*

David B. Givens, Centre for Non-Verbal Studies, 1999

I used to think that bereavement was a very sophisticated,
almost romantic, essentially human response 'grief for the loss
of love'. However, it is *not* the case that grieving is a sign of
fine feeling, higher sensitivity and advanced civilisation. It is a
raw, unhinged, animal activity.

John Bowlby, the authority on attachment and loss,
considered the research into bereavement reactions in animals
(geese, dogs, chimpanzees, orang-utans). He wrote in 'Processes
of Mourning' 1961 (*International Journal of Psychoanalysis*):

> *Members of lower species protest at the loss of a loved object
> and do all in their power to seek and recover it; hostility,
> externally directed is frequent; withdrawal, rejection of a
> potential new object, apathy and restlessness are the rule.*

Konrad Lorenz described what happened when a greylag goose
becomes separated from its mate:

> *The first response to the disappearance of the partner consists
> in the anxious attempt to find him again. The goose moves
> about restlessly by day and night, flying great distances and
> visiting places where the partner might be found, uttering all
> the time the penetrating trisyllabic long-distance call ... All
> the objective observable characteristics of the goose's behaviour
> on losing its mate are roughly identical with human grief.*

On Aggression, 1963,

The same automatic reaction happens to us when someone
important to us dies. Because we are so unused to having to
cope with such massive loss we have never learned how to
behave 'properly': our instinct takes over.

There are three conflicting biological responses.

◆ There is an impulse to call out loudly in a piercing scream
for the lost one so that they can be relocated: we'll seek out
places where they can usually be found and repeat the cry.

◆ There is, however, a conflicting impulse. We are frightened
and lonely: we have lost our protection so we don't want to
draw too much attention to our vulnerability.

◆ The result is that we *scream silently*. We breathe in deeply
and let out a stream of strangled, muted yelps. We sob.

The effect of forced expiration means that we need to protect
our eyes from excess pressure. To do this we will screw up our
face around the eyes – which will affect our tear ducts –
causing us to weep. (The same process happens in laughter but
then it's Ha! Ha! Ha! rather than Oh! Oh! Oh! – and there's no
worry about holding back.)

This wish to shout out loud very quietly can best be seen in
the mouth and throat. If you mime shouting as loud as you can
and then do nothing more than close your lips you will
reproduce exactly the feeling of a sob. (Notice that your eyes
will automatically have become screwed up.) You will feel the
strained muscles in your throat just as if you were sobbing.

Of course, it's not as simple as that. We don't sob and then
stop: we do it intermittently. It is as though we cry out in one
place, are satisfied there is no one there, but resume the
sobbing the next day when we go into the garden and find the
rosebush that she was going to plant – maybe she's here. These
are the recurrent 'pangs of grief'.

One of the by-products of this sobbing and weeping is that
other people have become used to recognising it as a signal of
extreme distress and an urgent call for help. Most people will
penetrate walls of social reserve to cross over the road to a
weeping stranger – 'Are you alright?' We all have the right to
make the appeal and we all have the duty to respond to it.

Grief is a tree that has tears for its fruit.

Philomen c.300 BC

When we burst into tears we almost inevitably say 'I'm sorry'.
What we mean is 'I apologise for choosing you to comfort me'.
The reply 'Don't worry about it' means 'It's OK, I accept your
appeal. I'm here to help in any way I can'. If someone replies
'Come on now – dry those tears' they're either embarrassed,
feeling inadequate (but still maybe wanting to help) or, less
commonly they mean to say 'Please stop signalling for help: I
don't want to be available'.

Maybe the raw crudity of extreme grief is why we can so
often find it embarrassing in ourselves and in others. We

normally go to great lengths to present ourselves as competent and responsible. When our 'adultness' is knocked aside by such overwhelming primitive feelings, it sparks off fears of being out of control – we are shocked by the prospect of chaos.

For this reason British grief is expressed very tentatively. Women tend to be less careful about showing their feelings compared to men whose past history has shown them that control is a vital tool of power. As we (men) gradually give up our need to be seen in control we will become less guarded about expressing vulnerability. (I wonder if one of the less welcome results of feminism will be that girls will grow up to appear as 'tough' as men.)

Some Eastern religious groups are much less inhibited about expressing grief. Perhaps their stronger sense of community support for individuals makes people more confident about appearing vulnerable and claiming the support of others.

Biologically, the beginning of the 'cure' for grief lies in recognising, admitting and describing our loss and having examined all parts of our life that were touched by the dead person finally admitting that they are definitely nowhere to be found. The search is called off.

> *Ophthalmologists are familiar with a condition called 'dry eye' – particularly common in older people who have been tearfully bereaved. There is a loss of the ability to weep. Whilst there's probably a straightforward physical reason for this, it remains a neat metaphor for the healing effect of tears.*
>
> Thomas Lambton

What can make grieving better or worse?

There are a variety of personal and life experiences, which can shape the path of our bereavement.

◆ *Our earlier grief experiences.* If we have had a particularly difficult bereavement in the past we will be tempted to associate how we felt then with how we feel now.

It need not have been a death – we may, for example, remember our parents divorcing when we were children or an elder sister moving away from home. The keenness of our loss from that time may become transferred to the present situation. We should ask ourselves what – precisely – our grief is about. It is almost certain that we will find loss more difficult later on if a parent died when we were children

◆ *Was it a sudden death?* There is a lot of evidence that, if we have time to adjust to someone's impending death we can settle 'unfinished business' and the process of grieving will have a better outcome.

◆ Similarly, *if the time leading up to the death was painful and protracted,* if the end was expected earlier and people were 'over-prepared' and exhausted by long periods of caring there will be a less satisfactory bereavement.

◆ *How much change will the death bring to our life?* If the only thing to change is the absence of the dead person, there is less to cope with. To handle our grief together with our children's sense of loss, a reduction in income or housing problems will make things much worse and our changed circumstances will forever remind us of the pain of that time. Our bereavement might become 'stuck'.

◆ *What sort of a person were we before?* If we were an anxious, dependent person before, we will have fewer inner resources to cope with the challenge of our loss. Similarly, if we have had poor physical or mental health we may have a bad time.

◆ *What was our relationship with the person?* If we were close we would have been able to share feelings and tie up loose ends. If we had a stormy, difficult relationship things will have been left unsaid and harsh feelings may be left hanging in the air. We may carry a burden of guilt that we could have behaved better.

The dying person will have a disappointing end to their life. If we are in such a situation it is clearly better to have put old quarrels behind us and to try to make some sort of reconciliation, perhaps with the help of someone else.

◆ *Particular categories of people are harder hit.* Men more than women: young people more than older people: bereaved parents more than anyone.

◆ *Are there other people around us for support?* It is common for even well-meaning friends to steer clear of bereaved people because they are sensitive to hurting them further by talking about their loss. This is usually not the real reason:

they may be embarrassed by the death and feel unable to find the right words.

The more contact with people who are comfortable about 'just being there', quietly giving practical help and wishing to listen, the better will be the grieving work.

◆ *Are there children or other dependent relatives involved?* It may be that the bereaved person is in such a state of shock that they are not able to give much attention to the children and their needs. They of course are in as much need of care as their surviving parent. If there is no support from others to help meet these needs, there may be extra distress to deal with in the future.

◆ The disbelief and unreality that may be in the air can be intensified *if the bereaved person has not been able to see the body.* If we have not seen the evidence there is always some hopeful mileage in our sad fantasy that they are not really dead. This is of course, all the more likely when there actually is no body – such as a drowning at sea. It sometimes takes much strength to face up to rational reality when we can conjure up comforting hope. On the other hand, there's maybe some wisdom in holding back our acceptance.

> *After the Vietnam War some women finally came to*
> *believe that their 'missing' husbands were actually dead.*
> *They went through the grieving process and dealt with their*
> *loss, only to have their husbands, who had been prisoners*
> *of war, released and returned to them. This may sound*
> *like a good plot for a Hollywood romance, but in reality*
> *this situation caused great difficulties for these couples and*
> *some of the marriages ended in divorce.*
> J. William Worden, *Grief Counselling and Grief Therapy,*
> Routledge 1993

◆ *Health before bereavement.* Illness can be worsened by the stress of grief and be a distraction.

◆ *Reduced material resources.* If there is sufficient money around many of the practical problems that arise can be avoided. Many people are forced into new responsibilities – arranging the funeral, driving, odd-jobs, decorating, housework – which could be set aside for the moment if temporary help could be bought. One writer concludes the most effective support to many bereaved people – more than any other form of support – would be an immediate government grant of £5,000.

◆ *Young widows*, in particular, are especially vulnerable to unusual emotional disturbance and often have periods of intense depression and persistent ill health. (Although the young bereaved are usually greatly distressed at first, they recover more successfully than older people who, on average, are less immediately affected, but slow to return to 'normal'.)

◆ *Personality factors.* People who will cope well are those who are emotionally stable, mature, conscientious, conservative (with a small c!), socially precise and optimistic. People who will cope less well are those who are emotionally unstable, with a negative outlook, apprehensive, worried or highly anxious.

◆ *Type of death.* 'Socially unspeakable' deaths, including suicide, murder, catastrophic circumstances, and 'stigmatised' deaths are harder to bear.

◆ *'Secret' deaths.* These are deaths – usually involving terminations of pregnancy or miscarriage, where, for whatever reason, there may be no public knowledge and therefore no sensitivity or support from family or friends.

◆ *Circumstances following the loss.* Other bereavements or other family or practical problems may distract us unhelpfully from our grieving and make recovery more difficult.

The four best predictors for recovery

◆ Initial effects of the bereavement: people who coped well at the time of the death recover much more quickly than people who had a very difficult time at the beginning.

◆ Good communication: people who were communicative with others about their thoughts and feelings tend to recover better.

◆ Positive self-esteem and personal skills: both these qualities are helpful to recovery.

◆ Time since the death: it is, indeed, a great healer.

Characteristics of successful grievers

Research (Ann Kaiser Stearns, *Coming Back*, Methuen 1989) amongst people who have coped particularly effectively with crisis and loss shows that they have particular traits.

◆ They will have anticipated the loss to some degree and imagined what the implications might be.

◆ When it's not possible to plan ahead they will identify with strong and resourceful people and learn from them. They may have inspirational role models to guide their attitudes.

◆ They prefer to turn away from negative, non-productive feelings and try to approach the situation without much complaint.

◆ Although they are personally resourceful, they are willing to seek help and support from others when needed. They know how to express their feelings freely and honestly.

◆ They are usually optimistic and they normally have an underlying need for personal growth and learning.

◆ They take responsibility for their own lives and 'own' their decisions: there is little inclination to look to others for blame.

◆ They are interested in regaining control of their situation following a crisis. They are prepared to analyse what has happened and make plans for what needs to be done.

◆ They tend to have a set of beliefs – not necessarily religious – which guides their life: a commitment to a set of principles by which they live.

◆ Even in the depths of early distress they can at times see humour when it is there: they can acknowledge the pain but don't take themselves too seriously – they are able to laugh at themselves.

◆ They try to see some possible positive gain in the outcome of the loss, either for themselves or others.

◆ They are determined people, prepared to put much energy into their recovery.

◆ They are able to be flexible, adaptable and imaginative about the future.

◆ They are at ease with themselves and the world as it is.

◆ They enjoy solving problems, restoring order and 'making things better'.

- They like being with other people who will tend to be positive-thinking.
- They look forward to the future more than they dwell in the past.
- They are able to let go of past resentments, regrets, guilt and injustices.

Women are better than men at grief?

The thing that sticks in my mind about Uncle Steven was that, the same afternoon of the day Auntie Judith died he went into the office to keep an appointment with a client (he was a solicitor). He said that contracts needed to be exchanged and . . . 'Life goes on.'

Margaret Ross

Of course men have losses in life – but we have less practice than women. As the sexes adopt more sensible, sharing roles, things will surely change, but traditionally women have had more than their fair share of loss. Because of their greater engagement with childcare and the family they have been hit harder than men. These losses seem cleverly spaced to give you just enough time to recover before the next one arrives.

- Loss of total dependence on a parent as a toddler.
- Loss of dependence on the family with the onset of adolescence.
- Loss of virginity in young adulthood.
- Loss of independence (and surname) on marriage.
- Loss of career after childbirth.
- Loss of children to school.
- Loss of grown-up children from home.
- Loss of ovulation and childbearing capacity.
- Loss of partner through (usual) pre-decease.

Older people who are bereaved will have learned to be men and women in the first half of the twentieth century. Gender differences then were usually much clearer.

Although there is a risk of stereotyping responses there are general differences in the way that men and women respond to emotional crises.

◆ He will tend to consider the broad situation. She will concentrate on the details.

◆ He may 'think' about the situation. She will focus on her feelings.

◆ He might try to be logical. She may rely on intuition.

◆ He may want to contain his emotions. She will want to express them.

◆ He may want to keep busy as a distraction. She will focus on her pain.

◆ He might avoid showing his feelings to strangers. She may welcome support from others.

◆ He might seek comfort and intimacy in sex. She may have no interest.

◆ He will tend to want things to get back to normal. She knows things will never be the same again.

To a lesser extent this will be generally true for people brought up in more recent years. The rapid changes in gender roles which we have seen in the last few decades will mean that there may be much less distinct grieving patterns in men and women in the future.

On the other hand we know so little about differences in the psychology of men and women. There is some evidence that the more straightforward, 'no nonsense' response seen so often in men may be a positive in-built genetic function, whose purpose is to ensure that 'life goes on'. Men's less demonstrative response also allows them to set aside their own feelings to look after their partner and ensure family survival.

Men will tend to approach loss with a wish to reorganise things and restructure family life. We do this because it involves a lot of thinking and planning and we may be biologically more comfortable with this. We will also have other characteristic responses:

◆ Remaining silent is a good protection against facing up to vulnerability.

◆ Experiencing solitary grief in private 'spares' others from seeing our pain. (There may be a lot of lengthy dog-walking.)

◆ Getting involved in activities – work, legal action, domestic support – will take up energy and thought: we won't have time to feel or reveal our pain.

We will be much happier with a 'problem-solving' approach and we'll be much more responsive to 'How did you react?' rather than 'How do you feel?'

Men and women seem to deal with their grief according to the strengths of their gender – this may be something to be celebrated rather than criticised.

> *Carl Jung says we balance our lives as we age... men become more in touch with their feminine qualities and women become more aggressive and in touch with their male qualities.*
>
> Ken Doka

If there is some truth in this we may need to hesitate before being critical of men's 'difficulty in looking at their feelings' – maybe (in spite of evidence to the contrary) masculine stoicism and apparent reluctance to grieve can be a normal and successful way of dealing with bereavement.

Unsurprisingly, research confirms that women show much greater distress after a bereavement and they are harder hit during the first year. They also seek medical and psychiatric help more readily.

Men, on the other hand, seem to cope well at first – although many more men than women will suffer a heart attack in the months after the loss of a partner. Another study (Young, Benjamin and Wallace, 1963) of 4,486 widowers over 54 revealed a 40 per cent increase in death rates during the six months following the death of a spouse.

Also, when men are followed up two to four years after the death they are usually found to have taken longer to recover than women. The general life expectancy of these widowers is reduced by 18 months as opposed to six months for widows and there is a 66-fold increase in suicidal deaths in widowers compared to a ten-fold increase for widows.

In a 1995 study of parents who had lost a baby it was concluded:

> *Mothers and fathers grieve differently: mothers grieve for their babies, fathers grieve for their wives.*
>
> Thomas and Striegel

Although there is much encouragement for men to express their feelings, paradoxically, when they do, there is some evidence that other people find it genuinely upsetting. The family – particularly the children – may find such vulnerability shocking in their father (it may also be the first time they have seen their father in tears).

Men in this situation are leaving the protector/provider role and the result is that the family experiences anxiety at the loss of that function. These men often quickly realise the discomfort of others with their tears, and this solidifies their solitary grief. In this way, men's so-called 'emotional immaturity' can be seen as simply a different, authentic and positive response.

Just because men cry less than women doesn't mean they feel less

The physical production of emotional tears is triggered by the hormone prolactin. Levels of this chemical drop at about the time a young boy enters adolescence. This makes it more difficult for men to access 'emotional' tears. This could have a genetic function – it may have been important for early Man not to reveal himself as vulnerable in the face of crisis.

> *... Another physical difference is provided by research, which indicates that men and women have significant differences in brain structure.*
>
> *One hypothesis theorises that this difference gives a woman a greater connection between her verbal capacity and her feelings, and leaves a man less able to verbalise feeling states. If this hypothesis is true, it would help explain why men tend towards* activity *in engaging their grief.*
>
> Tom Golden, *Swallowed by a Snake: The Gift of the Masculine Side of Healing*, 1999

Further research reveals that the network of connections in a woman's brain to do with communication amounts to 40 per cent of the total area: in men it's 7 per cent. Men sometimes find it easier to find a pathway to their grief through anger: women find it easier through sadness:

> *Many times in working with men I have found that while a man is expressing anger (and I mean really expressing it ... loudly, with movement of the body, etc.), he suddenly will be moved to tears. It is almost as if touching on that profound and deep feeling of anger has brought him in touch with his*

> *other feelings. This process is reversed with women. Many times a woman would be in tears, crying and crying. I might ask what her tears are about, and she often would state plainly and many times loudly 'I'm angry.'*
>
> Tom Golden, *Swallowed by a Snake: The Gift of the Masculine Side of Healing*, 1999

A further implication of these broad differences between men and women in their grieving needs is that we ought to expect different forms of support. To complain that 'men are notoriously bad at dealing with their feelings' is as unhelpful and offensive as to say 'women like to wallow in their feelings: they should get themselves more organised.'

Most of the material in this book will necessarily relate to women's grief, because it is much more visible, accessible and 'helpable': men will apparently cope well and be less vulnerable. However, some research, published as *The First Year of Bereavement* (Ira O. Glick, Robert S. Weiss and C. Murray Parkes, Wiley 1974) which contrasted widows with widowers came up with some other interesting results.

◆ Men tended to react to the traumatic disruption to their lives: women were more affected by the loss of the person.

◆ Men tended to think that they had lost 'part of themselves': women talked of loneliness and 'abandonment' by their dead partner.

◆ Men had more difficulty settling back into their working lives: for women work was often a helpful distraction.

◆ After a year 74 per cent of the women still cried occasionally as opposed to 40 per cent of the men.

◆ When they had some forewarning of their partner's death, men were better prepared: women tended not to want to believe it until it happened.

◆ Men were more 'realistic' in their attitude to their loss, showing fewer signs of hostility, injustice or disbelief.

◆ Men felt considerably more guilt about their own part in the time leading up to their partner's death but it was not long-lived: women felt less guilt but it lingered longer – and often increased.

◆ Men were twice as likely to have had 'involuntary visualisations' of their dead partners than women.

- ◆ Only a quarter of the men had talked with family or friends about their feeling as opposed to half the women.
- ◆ Men were seen by others as needing practical help because 'they couldn't do household tasks': women were supported so that they could 'attend to their feelings'.
- ◆ Men were all grateful for the help and support they received: women were sometimes critical.
- ◆ Only 4 per cent of the men had asked for professional help with their grief: with women the proportion was 40 per cent.
- ◆ Men were much less interested in the details of funeral arrangements and less satisfied with funeral directors.
- ◆ Men were more ready to seek a new partner sooner than women – sometimes after only a few months. However, they often brought their grief with them into their new partnership – causing further difficulties.
- ◆ Men who had been forewarned of their partner's death tended to adjust well to remarriage. Where the death had been unexpected they generally all had problems adjusting to a new relationship – but they tried. With women, the sudden death of their partner was much more likely to cause an almost phobic aversion to seeking another partner.

Men may need more active, practical ways of working with their grief. They don't want to be a burden to others, they want to maintain their independence, and they may want to 'be strong' in dealing with their grief. Unfortunately, the helping professions have traditionally been more familiar with working with women and the 'talking therapies' are consequently much more geared to looking at feelings. This not only may not be a successful way of helping men but it almost certainly discourages many men from seeking help.

The older, the easier?

Society avoids them, whether they are young or old, but especially if they are old, for in that case they are doubly distasteful. They have no one to talk to about the only subject that matters to them, the person they have lost.

Phillipe Aries, *The Hour of our Death*, 1983

We'll see later how difficult loss can be in a young family. Young people are unprepared for death and are often lacking emotional, social and material resources, which will add to their problems. The shock and intensity of grief are much more marked in young adults. However young people often have more resilience than the older generation, they can respond more easily to change and they have a stronger constitution in the face of the side effects on the immune system. The blow is greater but recovery is quicker and more successful.

We tend to neglect grief in older people. As we age we tend to slow down, be less active, become more reflective and more aware of our mortality. When someone close dies it may not be unexpected: they may have been incapacitated for some time and others may assume that their survivor is coping reasonably well – at least she may look as though she is.

Indeed there may not be so much of an immediate trauma. However, in a 1991 study *Grief in Elderly Adults* (Omega) Peter Sable found much greater levels of distress in older than younger widows if you asked them 'one to three years after their loss'. There are three good reasons for this:

◆ Longer relationships create greater dependence and, if they are unhappy, more regrets and greater opportunities for guilt.

◆ Older people are often less motivated to adapt to a new future.

◆ Our ability to respond to changes in our immune systems is reduced – leaving us open to physical symptoms of grief.

Bereavement in older people is, therefore, not as sharp initially but can be longer lasting and more problematic in the long run.

This is not to say that older people generally are not able to come through a bereavement successfully. Often age brings resilience, resourcefulness and stronger social supports. Even though over 70 per cent of bereaved older spouses reported the loss as the most stressful event of their lives, after two years over 80 per cent will be managing with a good degree of success.

Widowism

'Widow' is a harsh and hurtful word. It comes from the
Sanskrit and means 'empty'. I have been empty too long.
                                        Lynn Cain, *Widow*, 1974

'Widowism' describes an underlying attitude which is cloaked
in good intentions but which has a dark unconscious purpose.
It has been handed down through the years and, although no
one would agree with it these days, there is a danger that its
resonance lives on in our attitudes, not just to widows, but to
other bereaved people

If we look back on what has been written about grief, until
recent decades, it's mostly been by men describing women's
experience of bereavement. It tends to focus on the
'catastrophe' of the loss of her man and looks at ways in which
she can 'come to terms with her pain'.

The future lies in becoming used to her new life without
her all-important partner and finding what comfort she can in
her loneliness. It is describing the 'end' of a relationship and
paints a bleak picture of a pathetic victim who may be
fortunate enough (in exceptional circumstances) to be chosen
by another man for a new relationship – although the context
of age, lost social skills and poverty are also usually stressed.

Put this way – and I admit to some exaggeration – these are
plainly sexist and ageist attitudes. The unconscious intention is
to contain and remove an older woman – useless because of
her lack of male support – from social circulation.

All right, it's a far-fetched theory – but there's the smell of
truth in it.

Its deceptive appeal lies in its false logic: what greater
honour could there be to the quality of the lost relationship
than to declare it the most important, most unrepeatable
experience of our lives? What greater expression could there be
of our commitment than visibly to retire from life? To do
anything else might give the impression that we could imagine
something as good or better in the future.

Such an attitude might seem an exaggeration but it is
almost universally common. In rural Greece, for example, it is
the almost inflexible rule that a widow – even a young woman

– should dress from head to toe in black and shun all male attention for the rest of her life.

When we look at other important transitional stages in life – leaving home, getting married – they all leave enormous losses in their wake, but we don't dwell on what we've left behind: we see them as positive opportunities for development.

I'm not suggesting that the death of a lifelong partner could evoke any of the same hopes for the future but it seems a shame that there is such a universal social pressure on us to see only loss, failure, emptiness and hopelessness.

> *It was hard for her at first but it's good to see her out and about again. She's had her hair restyled and she's looking elegant. She's going to sell the business and start an aromatherapy consultancy with a friend. She misses their life together but says she feels ten years younger. It's all very exciting.*

That's someone talking about a friend six months after a divorce. Would it be unthinkable for a widow to talk in the same way?

Dr Morton Lieberman describes recent research he did with 700 widows and widowers.

> *I began this study with the typical mental health professional's attitude – a male perspective – which I have now come to understand was coloured by the myths and half-truths that I brought to the study. I started out thinking of widowhood as an illness and expecting that recovery would be the return to 'normality' – a life similar in most respects to the previous one. What I found, instead, were women who discovered in themselves a new way – a way of strength and assurance.*
>
> Doors Close, Doors Open: Widows Grieving and
> Growing, 1997

Change can bring about growth

> *Happiness is beneficial for the body, but it is grief that develops the powers of the mind.*
>
> Marcel Proust (1871–1922)

When I am dead, my dearest,
Sing no sad songs for me;
Plant thou no roses at my head,
Nor shady cypress tree...
And dreaming through the twilight
That doth not rise nor set,
Haply I may remember,
And haply may forget.

Christina Rossetti (1830–94), 'Song'

It is like being a budgie in a cage on a windowsill and finding
that someone has left the door open. No, we may not have
particularly enjoyed life in our cage, but we are used to it.
Now we have a decision to make. We can cower in a corner,
as far from the open door as possible; we can sit nervously just
by the open door, admiring the view without the bars and
imagining what it might be like outside; or we can attempt a
first tentative flutter.

Virginia Ironside, *You'll Get Over It!*, 1996

The deeper that sorrow carves into your being, the more joy
you will contain.

When you are joyous, look deep in your heart and you will
find it is only that which has given you sorrow that is giving
you joy.

When you are sorrowful look again into your heart, and you
will see that in truth you are weeping for that which has been
your delight.

Kahlil Gibran, *The Prophet*, 1926

How can there possibly be anything to be gained from the loss
of a loved one? We are used to seeing death being associated
with awkward and unremitting misery; it looks as though it
causes nothing but harm. However, some losses can develop
positive aspects.

'You just sit there and I'll see to that...'

One of the secret rewards of bereavement is that we are made
to feel special. We might be very cautious about admitting it
but this is a rare occasion when we can expect and demand the

attention and comfort of others. It's a seductive feeling (similar to the fuss we get when we're ill) because it takes us back to our childhood when we had our parents' unconditional love and support.

It's best that we accept this and resist any feeling of discomfort. Why not just yield to the interest and kindness of others? It is usually intended sincerely and likely to be useful.

On the other hand we might be more comfortable to be quiet and alone. If this is the case we should make our wishes clear: unwanted fuss can be very wearisome. (We might, however, have to cope with suspicions that we are 'avoiding things'.)

The other side of the coin, however, is that we may grow to like the attention far beyond the time when we actually need it. Fortunately, other people will let us know when we've 'outstayed our welcome'.

> *Grief is the agony of an instant: the indulgence of grief the blunder of a lifetime.*
>
> Benjamin Disraeli (1804–81), *Vivian Grey*

'We seem to have come closer together as a family...'

Although the focus is on the person who has died, the event brings together the immediate and the wider family – sometimes from a distance. The strengths and bonds of the family are reaffirmed and honest feelings are revealed which can deepen relationships: often, positive feelings emerge unexpectedly. (On the other hand, if they are the 'wrong' sort of honest feelings there can be family havoc.)

On the whole bereavement will tend to unite and mature a family. The surviving partner may think that it is the end of their world, but it isn't. Just as the harshness of the winter gives way to spring, so we, if our bereavement has been successful, will eventually emerge from the worst of our grieving and realise the possibilities for the future.

'You've only got yourself to think of now...'

Maybe for the first time in our life we can put ourselves first. Long-term family relationships can be very satisfying, but to sustain them we may have set aside some of our personal needs over a long period of years.

We would never have chosen it this way, but we can now reassess personal goals: there may even be life insurance money to help us on our way.

> *For the last 11 years Phillip was in a wheelchair and before that the children were at home, so I'd never even considered putting what I wanted first. I thought I was perfectly content – I never resented being a carer.*
>
> *Although expected, it was still a shock when he died. For months after I was at a loose end. One day my sister jokingly suggested Greece. She reminded me how, as a teenager, I had been passionate about Greek mythology and used to dream of going there.*
>
> *Gradually the idea began to form in my mind and I began to feel excited for the first time in years. The following year I spent four months touring archaeological sites and museums in Greece and Crete. It changed my life. I made new friends and I'm going back to Athens for three months in September.*
>
> Margery Lambert

Often, after living a rather dull, uneventful life, bereavement can act like an electric shock to force us to confront our future directly and look for a purpose in it. Our old way of life has been swept away and we can't avoid facing the basic questions:

◆ 'Why do I wish to continue living?'
◆ 'What will I do now?'

At first our response to these questions may be negative and it would be better to put them to one side. However, they won't go away: eventually we're going to have to respond to them.

Many people, who can eventually come to accept their loss, will realise that there is a possibility of a new, different future, full of meaning and richness.

> *People who have had entirely happy marriages may often find, even in the middle of feeling unhappy, a weird sense of freedom when their partner dies, a feeling of release from being conjoined to another person. They are suddenly aware of how much their personality was buried or enmeshed with the*

*other's ... many is the man who suddenly finds that his wife
has been keeping the joys of cooking from him for years, or the
woman who delights in suddenly taking charge of everything
and thrills at last to be in the driving seat of the car.*

Virginia Ironside, *You'll Get Over It!*, 1996

*It is one of life's laws that as soon as one door closes, another
opens. But the tragedy is that we look at the closed door and
ignore the open one.*

Andre Gide

'It's a lesson for all of us...'

*I walked a mile with Pleasure;
She chattered all the way.
But left me none the wiser
For all she had to say.
I walked a mile with Sorrow
And ne'er a word said she;
But oh, the things I learned from her
When Sorrow walked with me!*

Robert Browning (1812–89), 'Along the Road'

Another pay-off is the simple realisation of the reality of death
and the uncertainties of life – how we should value the present:
death can come to anyone at any time: a bitter but maturing
experience.

What would have been left unsaid to whom if you were to
die in an hour's time? What will you regret not having said to
whom if they die tomorrow? As Elisabeth Kübler-Ross writes:

*What I try to teach people is to live in such a way that you
say those things while the other person can still hear them.*

If we have made the journey through bereavement we will also
be in a good position to help others through their grief:

*The more people have lost, the more they will eventually have
– to offer others.*

Dr Colin Murray Parkes, *Recovery from Bereavement*,
1983

Working through the chaos and pain of bereavement is hard, but can be productive. The effort can have spin-offs, which can help us move into a more developed level of functioning.

> *By facing despair, and not succumbing, they know their inner capacities in a more complete way. These gains do not in any way diminish the fact of the loss. But yes they are benefits. Dearly purchased, hard earned benefits.*
>
> S. A. Schwartzberg, *A Crisis of Meaning*,
> Oxford University Press 1996

Case study: Anna and Stephanie

When Anna's partner Stephanie died just before her 61st birthday, Anna was desolate. They had been together for 35 years and they had been very close. Stephanie had been a well-known and successful architect and was very much the dominant partner. Anna had always been timid and submissive and Stephanie had wanted her to remain in the background. In the early days, homosexuality was not spoken about, and Stephanie had encouraged the assumption that she lived alone.

When Stephanie went out socially Anna would stay at home. Because of her prosperity Stephanie persuaded Anna to give up her work in the library in the 1970s: she liked her new found domesticity at first, but after a few years she became bored – not seriously enough to complain to Stephanie though: her aim was always to please her friend. For the last 25 years she devoted her life to Stephanie, sacrificing any personal ambition.

Stephanie had drowned in a boating accident. She hadn't made a will and her total estate went to her aged father (Anna could have contested the decision but she couldn't bring herself to make their relationship public). She kept away from the funeral for fear of showing her distress and revealing their closeness. So it was that on a rainy October morning the Birmingham flat sold – she found herself with a large trunk and a suitcase on Euston Station. She had no friends, little money and she was estranged from her family. She had little financial sense and few social skills: she felt vulnerable and frightened.

She managed to get an administrative job in the library of the Royal College of Architects – she had learned a lot about architecture over the years. She discovered that she had retained her good organisational skills and extra responsibility gave her increased confidence. She tentatively became a familiar member of the lesbian community and began a new relationship with someone who reminded her of her former, timid self.

After a couple of years she became office manager of the Home Counties Lesbian Helpline. Today she is the director. She's working on a biography of Anna. _____

'It's like a bereavement...'

While we're thinking about the nature of grief it's worth remembering that bereavement is not some special set of feelings connected only with death. It's to do with loss *or* sudden change.

Any important loss will carry its own quota of grief.

◆ We can grieve for our own physical loss if we become disabled.

◆ Sudden poverty can cause economic bereavement.

◆ Redundancy or retirement may cause us to feel bereaved of our work routine and sense of ourselves.

◆ Many separations – where there may be accompanying feelings of failure and bitterness – can have more impact on us than if our partner had died.

◆ We can celebrate our lottery win, but we may also grieve for our old, familiar way of life.

◆ Some degenerative diseases – Alzheimer's Disease for example – feature total or intermittent loss of personality, causing confused grief for a living person – 'For me, my mother died two years ago...'

◆ So-called 'mid-life crises' are often simply grief for the loss of our own unfulfilled ambitions – 'This is as good as it's going to get.'

◆ Theft or lost property can cause us what seems disproportionate distress.

It isn't *like* a bereavement: it *is* a bereavement.

CHAPTER 3

When Things Go Wrong

W e tend to think of bereavement as a time of quiet feelings of loss, withdrawal and sadness, but underlying this the ravages of stress are at work.

The physical damage of grief

We are faced with catastrophe and our 'fight or flight' impulse comes into play. This has the physiological effect of mobilising our body for immediate action but there is no one to fight and nowhere to run. Our body, however, remains poised for action, diverting resources from other – inessential for the moment – parts. Thus deprived, the performance of our brains, hearts, digestive and reproductive systems is reduced and their inefficiency soon begins to show. These effects can show themselves in all sorts of ways:

- dizziness
- rashes
- shivering
- sore throat
- dry mouth
- diarrhoea
- insomnia
- emptiness
- weight loss
- over-eating
- flu symptoms
- indigestion
- jumpiness
- memory lapses
- nightmares
- impotence

- headaches
- sweating
- nausea
- muscle pains
- constipation
- panic attacks
- irritability
- clamminess
- stomach pain
- palpitations
- loss of appetite
- feeling sick
- noise intolerance
- vision problems
- no concentration
- menstrual problems.

These symptoms can be made worse by poor nutrition, the sheer pressure of distress and the speed of events.

The 'fight or flight' impulse harks back to prehistory when our underdeveloped, simple brains responded to difficult situations by hitting out or running away. 'Doing' something as quickly as possible was all we knew in those days – there was no question of 'talking things through' with a tiger. This action-readiness saved many lives then. Nowadays, we're more civilised and sophisticated: we all know that cowardice and rash displays of aggression are ill-advised.

Nevertheless we're stuck with veinfuls of switched-on chemicals which won't go away until they've been used. They don't respond to 'thinking', 'talking' or 'understanding'. They only know how to do things 'now!'. They 'helpfully' divert all our energy away from all parts of the body which are not immediately necessary for aggression or escape.

The trouble is that when we choose not to use this energy the impulse remains: our muscles remain obsessively tensed for action to the increasing detriment of the rest of our bodies. This strained tension and increasing risk of illness is stress – and it won't go away unless we do something about it.

If we could find the energy, we could get rid of much of the tension very quickly with vigorous exercise. The trouble is that stress can be exhausting and 'paralysing', and in our early grief we have no interest in 'feeling better'.

Sometimes, our reaction to a death is so overwhelming that we just can't summon *any* resources to deal with it. For a while we can't cope with the fact – it becomes literally 'unthinkable'. It's as though all our physical and mental processes are so overloaded that our whole body 'blows a fuse' and we are temporarily lost to reality. To an outsider this can appear very serious and worrying but it is a natural, self-protective process from which we'll eventually emerge.

Mostly these physical effects are temporary and we recover. Whilst there is little evidence that an important loss can lead directly to increased general mortality in the survivor there is some evidence that – especially among older widowers – severe grief can lead to increased cardio-vascular disease. Grief has also been associated with:

- ◆ glaucoma
- ◆ rheumatoid arthritis
- ◆ pneumonia
- ◆ stomach ulcers

- ◆ cancer
- ◆ pernicious anaemia
- ◆ tuberculosis
- ◆ ulcerative colitis.

There is also an underrated risk that depression that is not dramatically evident can continue and grow imperceptibly to become a chronic, untreated, lifelong disability.

Finally one of the other physical effects of grief is, quite simply, death. This is not a serious risk factor but, nevertheless, when stress, depression, illness and lack of support come together we may, indeed, just fade away. There is clear evidence that links a higher death rate from heart disease in older men to bereavement.

'Of course I'll miss him – in spite of everything'

> *The intensity of your grief is a measure of the seriousness of your loss, not a measure of the virtue of the one who has died. Your loss has to do with many things beside that. The one who has died has not suddenly become a saint.*
> Dr R. M. Youngson, *Grief: Rebuilding Your Life after a*
> *Bereavement,* 1989

The hurt of grief is about the loss of our investment in the relationship with the person who has died. It matters little what sort of a person they were – saintly, abusive, reliable, criminal. We can accommodate ourselves to anybody if our needs are being met. The value that we put on this investment is intangible, hard to describe – and a little bit selfish – so there is a temptation to transfer its importance to the person themself.

People may mistakenly think that we will be 'better off' if a partner in an abusive, 'bad' relationship dies – especially if it has gone on for years. They will find it hard to acknowledge that we are nevertheless deeply bereaved. Even in such apparently negative relationships, however, we may have given a massive (but wasted) emotional commitment. Such a relationship may have damaged our confidence and sense of independence, reducing our capacity to face the freedom of life on our own.

Faced with feelings of failure and guilt we may be tempted into re-inventing the relationship – reconstructing it for our own comfort and the estimation of others as successful and close, 'but misunderstood'.

Somehow we have the idea that we can only be bereft of someone if they were 'good': that we can only grieve for a relationship that was positive. In fact, if it was a long-lasting 'partner' relationship, no matter how you measure its *quality*, its *quantity* filled much of our lives and it is the 'hole' left by its loss that we are dealing with.

> *One couple, in their sixties, were constantly bickering and finding fault with each other. They were childless, lived alone, had no friends and had always rejected contact with the neighbours. Their marriage seemed to be held together with a thread.*
>
> *When the wife died, the husband fell to pieces. His abusive wife had caused him nothing but distress during most of their 40 years together. But their marriage was all he had. He died 15 months later.*
>
> Thomas Lambton

The most unlikely people are suddenly canonised in death: past injuries are forgotten and only good things remembered. This editing of experience is mostly harmless, especially as it goes along with the generally useful accepted injunction 'never to speak ill of the dead'. The trouble starts when we use our idealised version of the dead person to manipulate the living:

◆ 'Your brother would never have done that...'
◆ 'You'll never be as successful as your father...'
◆ 'Your mother may have beaten you, but it was only for your own good...'

Not only will such fantasies be unconvincing and resented by people who know what the reality was, but we will run the risk of fooling ourselves and becoming trapped by confusing memories.

The hidden dangers of grief

> *There is now a very general recognition that human beings*

have sexual urges and that, if these are denied outlet, the result
will be suffering – either psychological or physical or both. But
there is no analogous secular recognition of the fact that
human beings mourn in response to grief, and that, if
mourning is denied an outlet, the result will be suffering –
either psychological or physical or both.

Geoffrey Gorer, *Death, Grief, and Mourning in*
Contemporary Britain, 1965

An important loss may leave us vulnerable.

◆ The disruption to our life may lead us to feel that we need to 'do' something. There may be an impulse to get rid of clothes and possessions with their associated memories; we may associate our changed future with a sudden impulse to move house. Our ability to make sound decisions is suspended – we will hopefully have people around us to restrain our rash impulses.

◆ Recovery from the bruises of loss is not helped by further changes that may lead us towards further distress: now is not the time to rush into another relationship.

◆ Similarly we should guard against – or be protected from – uncharacteristic behaviour. Our thought processes may be skewed by the stress we are experiencing and we may act more from instinct than good judgement.

◆ We may horrify others and ourselves by acting out of character; confused feelings of anger might be expressed in obscenities.

◆ Our need for comfort might take us on a massive shopping spree; our distorted sense of physical loss of a partner might plunge us into an ill-judged casual sexual adventure.

◆ In order to grieve, we've got to be able to love. We might – having suffered the grief – decide it's not worth loving again. It is.

◆ To suffer the lasting, impotent pain of grief is to become a 'victim'. Many people find some relief from this role by inflicting pain on others: there's a comforting sense of control. It's more respectable, however, to gain this satisfaction – such as it is – not by hurting others, but by harming ourselves. The choice is ours: drugs, over-eating, sexual promiscuity or some other reckless behaviour.

- More likely we might increase our use of alcohol – this may develop into an unwise habit if its anaesthetic effects become associated with our melancholy.
- We may become irrationally overprotective of family members.
- We may experience frightening or violent nightmares involving the person who has died.
- We may think all meaning has gone from life and we may fantasize about suicide.
- We may resent happiness in other people which may make us uncharacteristically spiteful.

Following shortly after a death such out-of-place behaviour can easily be seen for what it is. In the months that follow, however, when we feel we are recovering, we may begin to feel, wrongly, that we are more in control.

It is easy to overestimate our fitness for making wise decisions – especially if we have been used to sharing plans with our dead partner. We may, by then, need to make decisions about how to dispose of our partner's estate: we should guard against the advice of others and our own passing whims.

The deep sense of loss may drive us towards the intimacy of sex, as explained by one man in his late forties:

> *We'd slept together every night for the last 18 years. I just ached to put my arms around her and feel her beside me.*
>
> *After a couple of weeks I realised I was also missing our sex together. I eventually picked someone up and we made love. I felt awful – it seemed so disloyal. Anyway, we saw each other a few more times but it had to end: she wanted more but, for me, it had just been sex.*

Fred Michaels

If it feels right, we should not feel guilty about having strong sexual feelings. This can be a taboo area because sex is so commonly associated with happy carefree times. However, many people see sex as a way of releasing tension and it can become a way of coping with the unbearable parts of life – like grief. It can also be a natural way to receive comfort from the pain and distress.

The death and our retreat from social life may make us feel lonely and isolated. We may have conflicting ideas about our future.

◆ 'How can I possibly consider another relationship after the one I have lost.'
◆ 'I fantasize about finding someone just like her: it would be as though nothing has happened.'
◆ 'The sensible thing would be to put things behind me and start a new life and a fresh relationship.'
◆ 'What will it say about my lost relationship if I can replace it so quickly and completely.'

If we have children they may well have strong views about our 'betrayal' of their mother or father.

Whatever we do, the quicker and more impulsively that we do it, the more potentially dangerous will be the outcome. It's unwise, usually, to have hard and fast rules but it's a good rule of thumb to take a year out before making any major decisions. It's interesting that the traditional idea of a formal lengthy period of mourning, whilst dwelling perhaps overly on the negative aspects of loss, did allow for this time of regeneration.

The word quarantine is derived from the Italian 'quarantina' which referred to the 40 day period that a widow was sequestered from the world.

Thomas Lambton

*She saw the rest
of her life as a
bad debt to be
discharged.*
LADY CYNTHIA
ASQUITH, 1915

CHAPTER 4

When We Could Do With Some Help

Although when it happens to us it may seem at first that we shall never recover, the vast majority of bereaved people emerge naturally from the sharpness of their grief with the normal support of family and friends.

About 10 per cent of people, however, will have complications, which may require more specialised help. The main reasons are:

- the normal grieving process becomes stuck and the grief becomes chronic and disabling
- the response to the death is delayed and is replaced by an ever-deepening depression and withdrawal
- with some people their chronic grief may also have been delayed in its onset.

Bereft forever: chronic grief

Many people whose grief will not subside may have persistent, continuing symptoms:

- insomnia
- panic attacks
- social isolation
- irrational outbursts
- loss of self-esteem
- recurrent ill health.

Whilst the 'normal' grieving time is very variable – a few months to several years, the *chronic* griever is easily identified – the *intensity* of their grief has not *reduced* over a long period of time.

They may show the same reactions as at the time of the death but there is an added component – they have no sense of wishing to move forward through their bereavement. Indeed, this may make other people feel that they are being self-indulgent – 'wallowing in their sorrow'.

This may be true to some extent as overgrown grief is usually fed by impulses of guilt and self-punishment. Unfortunately, the eventual impatience of those around them only makes such people more withdrawn and helpless.

When normal grief is extended in this way, the (normally brief) symptoms can become exaggerated. There can be:

◆ an intense preoccupation with thoughts of the dead person
◆ loss of emotional control
◆ occasional violent outbursts
◆ thoughts of suicide
◆ neglect of other aspects of life.

What is usually the healthy expression of fresh grief becomes with time morbid and obsessive.

The preoccupation with self-punishment will give no encouragement to seek assistance but it is at this stage – when things have become a black, vicious circle – that skilled help may be most needed.

If we get stuck in this way we need someone else gently to question our obsessions and coax us back to a positive reality. We can't be advised, persuaded or cajoled; we need to be encouraged to look at our thoughts, feelings and memories and to talk about them to someone wanting to understand (and listen). We need to decide for ourselves how far our perception measures up to reality.

It's usually a question of being able to be honest, respectful and forgiving about the dead person, other people and ourselves. Unsurprisingly, we are usually hardest on ourselves.

> *Why should I sorrow for what was pain;*
> *A cherished grief is an iron chain.*
>
> Stephen Vincent Benet, 'King David'

Grief postponed

About a third of us who have serious problems with bereavement, far from being preoccupied with our loss, postpone our grief.

It is as though we refuse to acknowledge what has happened and, unconsciously, protect ourselves (for a time) against the prospect of grief pain.

'I don't think it's penetrated fully yet...'

Here, our reactions may appear unfeeling and bizarre to others, who will be perplexed about how to respond to us. We may appear emotionally flat and apparently able to get on easily with day-to-day life, concentrating on work, keeping busy – 'changing the subject' of the death.

However, we can only sustain the delusion for a certain amount of time – hours, days, weeks, sometimes years... Either we come to accept what has happened, in our own time and in our own terms, or we can slip into a dangerous depression. 'Dangerous' because it can be mistaken for grief and, untreated, it could linger indefinitely. Some people never recover.

There are a few people, however – mostly men – who have the ability to set their feelings aside successfully and just get on with their lives. If this is causing them no problems, it is perfectly acceptable; we shouldn't be critical of them or seek to probe their feelings – there is a wide range of healthy bereavement.

Exaggerated grief

> ... my particular grief
> Is of so flood-gate and o'erbearing nature
> That it engluts and swallows other sorrows.
>
> Shakespeare, *Othello*

In a sense all grief seems an exaggeration of feeling, but this complication refers to those situations where 'ordinary' bereavement becomes overlaid with other complex symptoms.

◆ Serious psychiatric disorders – not the predictable, normal, transient depression caused by loss, but a full-blown psychotic disorder needing expert attention.
◆ Neuroses: panic attacks and phobias.

- Alcoholism or other substance abuse.
- Post-traumatic stress disorder.

All these conditions can appear unrelated to the original grief that may have been behind them. However, they could be hard to deal with if they are not seen in the context of loss.

Guilty grief

Where we have a very close relationship with someone, we are important to them and we have many opportunities to influence their lives. Because our lives touch theirs so often we can, if we choose, always find some way in which we could have prevented their death.

'We killed him – me and the hospital...'

In many situations our analysis may be logically (if not morally) correct.

> *If I hadn't provoked the row, he wouldn't have stormed out of the house so blindly and he may not have been hit by the motorbike.*

Here, we need to own up squarely to the unfortunate truth and be able to forgive ourselves. Hard, but possible.

More often, however, where we feel bad about our part in the relationship our imagination will go out of its way to manufacture some half-credible self-accusation.

> *If I'd only encouraged her more to go to the doctor's when she first began to have the headaches...*

Good sense and the passage of time will give us a more rational perspective on the level of our 'blame'. Sometimes, however, it seems we almost go to extremes to defy rationality.

> *If I hadn't wanted to retire to the seaside, he would never have drowned...*

This separates cause and effect so far that it defies logic. Because it is also (very, very) remotely true (he probably wouldn't actually have had the opportunity of falling into the docks) we can remain unchallenged and firmly locked inside this sort of guilt for ever.

It's not that we are unable to work our own way out of the impasse, it's just – as with other sorts of grief problems – that we can quickly become enveloped in a self-generating cocoon of inward-looking thoughts and feelings that conspire to shut out reality.

This is when a stranger or a friend, less affected by the loss, can help us recognise for ourselves what our feelings and behaviour mean. They can bring in some worldly reality and stand by us as we look to the future.

Depression

All grief causes a certain degree of normal depression. This will usually clear over a period of time and we and those around us will notice gradual improvements. Sometimes, however, the despair following a death can become transformed into a psychiatric disorder which can be identified by a gradual deterioration in our mood over the weeks following the death.

How depressed are you?

Read the following statements about how you may have been feeling over the last few days. If your bereavement is very recent it may be perfectly normal to experience all these feelings. However, if you can detect no improvement at all as time goes on it may be worth seeking medical help.

1. 'The future seems empty to me.'
2. 'I find it hard to concentrate for more than a few minutes.'
3. 'I've stopped caring about things that were once important to me.'
4. 'Things have slowed down for me.'
5. 'I can no longer take pleasure in life.'
6. 'I feel constantly tired.'
7. 'I don't seem to be able to make decisions any more.'
8. 'It takes ages for me to do the simplest thing.'
9. 'I feel miserable.'
10. 'I feel guilty and I deserve feeling bad about things.'
11. 'I feel cornered and unable to escape.'
12. 'I have a feeling of emptiness.'

13. 'I have difficulty getting to sleep, staying asleep or waking up.'
14. 'I can't settle – I've always got to be "on the move".'
15. 'Methods of killing myself are on my mind.'
16. 'I have put on (or lost) weight for no apparent reason.'
17. 'I feel a failure.'
18. 'There is nothing that can make me feel better.'

Adapted from the
Goldberg Depression Inventory, 1993

The ten clues to trouble ahead

The following factors may all to some degree be part of the normal grieving process. However, research has shown that if they continue unabated – and especially if they increase rather than decrease – we may be having difficulties in our bereavement.

◆ We can't speak about the dead person without experiencing intense, fresh distress – even after months or years. This may even happen when we hear someone else talking about their own grief.

◆ We constantly dwell on other, apparently unrelated, loss situations.

◆ Our unwillingness to move the possessions of the dead person or determination to keep their room 'exactly as he left it'.

◆ We watch out for any (phantom) physical symptoms similar to those of the dead person's terminal illness: these can become particularly evident on the anniversary of the death.

◆ We can assume characteristics and personality traits of the dead person – maybe an unconscious attempt to keep them alive in us.

◆ We might make dramatic changes to our lifestyle: moving house, excluding ourselves from friends and familiar activities – cutting ourselves off from all connection with the dead person, as though we are trying to pretend that all trace of them is lost.

◆ We are unwilling to have anything to do with the funeral rituals or we refuse to visit the grave.

◆ We experience chronic, worsening depression or its opposite

– sustained false euphoria.
◆ We entertain thoughts of self-harm or suicide.
◆ We develop an obsessive phobia or irrational fear of the disease that led to the death.

How others can help us (and how we can help others)

Give sorrow words; the grief that does not speak
Whispers the o'er-fraught heart and bids it break.

Shakespeare, *Macbeth*

Your logic, my friend, is perfect,
Your moral most drearily true;
But since the earth clashed on her coffin,
I keep hearing that, and not you.

James Russell Lowell (1819–91), *After the Funeral*

The trouble with most other people is that they aren't used to bereavement.

A hundred years ago it was usual for death to be much more evident. There weren't the knowledge or resources to treat disease effectively so death had an inevitability about it. Those of us who are older will remember the real concern of grandparents for our slightest sign of illness as a child – when they said we should wear a scarf and gloves they knew what they were talking about.

Death did not – as it does today – belong to the doctors; people were cared for and died in the midst of their families, friends and neighbours. Most deaths now happen in hospitals in antiseptic isolation. Bodies are kept away from home – apart from the funeral, death is generally invisible.

Nowadays, extended families are much less likely to live closely together in strong relationships. People move jobs and close friendships dwindle: there is less intimacy and interdependence with our neighbours.

Most people will experience only a couple of significant bereavements in their lifetime – our Victorian ancestors would have known dozens. Because we're preoccupied with our grief at these times our understanding of what is happening is blunted – perhaps the only thing we learn is that death is distressing. When we come across other grieving people in future, because of our inexperience, we are unlikely ever to have learned enough about how they are likely to be feeling.

We are usually nervous of dealing with strong, negative emotions in other people – and we fear that some bereavement feelings can be very 'dangerous'.

◆ We shy away from having to deal with uncommon, exaggerated feelings.

◆ We may feel that we are being drawn into an unfamiliar, socially inappropriate closeness with someone.

◆ We feel lost for words – any distress seems to demand that we say something which will relieve it.

◆ We are keenly aware of the person's vulnerability and we fear that our stumbling response may make matters worse.

◆ The distress may seem so serious that it requires urgent professional help rather than our incompetent meddling.

Bereavement is not a disease requiring skilled diagnosis, treatment and supervision. It is a normal response to a death and will mostly be best contained within a circle of family and friends. When someone experiences a severe loss the greatest support they can have is in the security of continuing close relationships. The last thing they need is for a professional stranger to move in and begin to assess and analyse the situation. There may come a time – for a few people whose grieving has been complicated by other problems – where counselling or medical help is needed, but this will be rare.

Much is needed to bring us grief – little to console us.
Jean Rostand (1894–1977), *Journal d'un Caractère*

We need someone who will 'be' with us and keep a channel open to our feelings. It's not at all a simple process, but successful mourning seems to involve us in:

◆ fully recognising and acknowledging our own pain

◆ translating the raw feelings into accurate words

◆ transmitting the description to someone else

◆ someone else 'hearing' the expressed feelings

◆ then, the other person showing the griever that the feelings have been correctly understood.

We need to be able to *communicate* our grief for it to be acknowledged. It's not just our general sense of loss that needs to be made known but, crucially, those special aspects that make it particular to us. Nobody can understand exactly how we feel without having heard precise details of our loss.

> *For grief, once told, brings somewhat back of peace.*
> William Morris (1834–96), *The Earthly Paradise*

Just why it is that there is some healing magic in this communication exchange is unclear: it's as though the pain is reduced when the feelings are 'displayed' expressed and acknowledged by someone else.

Tears produce a similar effect: the pain seems capable of being liquefied in the tear ducts and expressed through the eyes.

> *Sorrow, like a river, must be given vent, lest it erode the bank.*
> Mexican proverb

> *It's just the pain coming out of your eyes.*
> Anna Raeburn, Talk Radio, 1999

Rules for helping bereaved people

> *When we do communicate our feelings after a bereavement, if we don't get silence or fear, we almost certainly get the wrong response. Eighty per cent of the time you receive what is a verbal slap in the face – all the worse because it's not intended as such: it's intended as kindness.*
> Virginia Ironside, *You'll Get Over It!*, 1996

We don't have to find some solution for relieving the distress. In fact, making suggestions and offering advice is curiously restrictive. We are there to be used as they think fit – a pair of ears and an alert mind to receive their thoughts and feelings. Proposing 'solutions' is an interference. (In any case, there aren't any 'solutions'.)

We are not there as some sort of safety net to prevent the distress deepening. The pain is always keenest at the beginning and will always tend to lessen and be self-corrective as the meaning of the situation becomes clearer for the mourner. A positive emotional climate will allow them to come up with their own, productive answers.

Don't walk in front of me, I may not follow.
Don't walk behind me, I may not lead.
Walk beside me and just be my friend.

Albert Camus (1913–60)

The better we can just listen, the more we will encourage them to talk usefully. We all make sense of shocked, confused feelings by turning them into thoughts – usually in the privacy of our own minds. The most positive grief work usually comes about by being 'invited' to put these thoughts into spoken words: any sloppiness or vagueness in our thinking is challenged by us having to find the right words to express them.

To have someone listen to us encourages us to be even more precise. When that person shows an interest in understanding precisely what we are feeling it can give some shape and reality to any vagueness or uncertainty. An added luxury is for the listener to be alert to things we say which are inconsistent or contradictory and gently to check out exactly what we mean. They may also notice our non-verbal behaviour and what we significantly omit.

For the listener none of this is difficult. We are little more than a friendly tape recorder which takes some pride in recording precisely what is being said and experienced, and then playing it back authentically. The bereaved person may hear things for the first time that he didn't know he felt or knew.

As long as we are genuinely interested, positive and willing to give time and attention; and so long as we don't bring too many of our own concerns into the conversation, we can all do it.

The trouble is that we so rarely see it done. Our experience of 'counselling' comes from dramatic psychological thrillers where we see wise psychiatrists with an apparently faultless understanding of human psychology. They seem to understand their patient better than he does himself and are able to come up with the exact form of words which will produce a miracle cure.

Such situations may or may not occur in real life (I suspect they never do). It's important to know that this process has normally nothing to do with the needs of bereaved people. The psychiatrist or professional counsellor takes some responsibility for taking charge of the 'treatment' in rare situations where worsening problems are intense and deeply rooted.

We as listeners are *never* in charge: we don't interfere, manipulate, analyse or impose solutions. The bereaved person is *always* in charge and all the 'work' is done by them. Our only responsibility is to notice if things are getting steadily worse when we may wish to ask if more skilled help is needed.

Gradually, the bereaved person will be able to refocus their thoughts and feelings as they see things in a different perspective: the initial catastrophe will slowly gain a new meaning.

But what can we say to help someone's grief

> *If you want to drive yourself crazy, try to figure out what other people want you to be. And then try to become it. A perfect recipe for self-destruction.*
>
> Susan Jeffers, *Thoughts of Power and Love*, 1997

It's important to realise that there is *no need* to make suggestions or give advice. The main qualification is a genuine unselfish willingness to give our time and attention; most mature adults can do this. Often 'experts' make a mess of it – their professional 'responsibility' can interfere with the simple humanity required.

> *Nothing speaks our grief so well*
> *As to speak nothing.*
> Richard Crashaw (1612–49), 'On the Death of Mr Herrys'

Because there is no responsibility on us to 'guide' conversation, we can take pauses – even long ones – in our stride. We should allow the style and pace of conversation to be set by the person doing the grieving.

It's sometimes helpful to give an assurance that tears are OK: that you expect them as a natural expression of grieving. You want her to feel comfortable and relaxed about weeping – it's important that we should show that emotion is not going to upset us.

Expect and accept that the survivor will retell details of

events and repeat a description of their feelings. This might feel at first as though things are going in circles but repetition can be creative:

> *I must have been a real bore. The number of times I went over the details of the accident with Clemmie!...But she stayed and put on a brave face. But the more I talked about what happened then and what would happen now, the easier it became and the less frantic I felt...*

Cecily Calder

One of the most valuable – and difficult – things we can do for survivors is simply to be patient. People in distress are sometimes irrational, obsessive or unreasonably critical and there may be a temptation to be drawn into 'putting the record straight'. It may satisfy us to do this but it's unlikely to be very helpful to someone whose thinking is askew. We'd do better to set aside our own feelings as listener and stay with theirs: things will eventually subside.

With so much pain about, it's easy to be caught up in the distress and gloom. However, one of our functions when supporting someone in grief is to keep alive the possibility of recovery. We need to acknowledge their sadness but it is doing them no favours to conspire with their hopelessness and negative view of the world. As far as possible we should try to maintain a positive perspective on the situation. We can do this by keeping alive the memory of their previous interests and moving the focus into the future. It's a difficult balance to achieve.

We should prevent our own experiences from intruding. We may genuinely think that to hear about our 'even more tragic' bereavement last year will help bring some hope and proportion to the situation. However, our experiences, although relevant, can come across as irrelevant, disabling and curiously impertinent.

If we feel some difficulty about talking to someone face to face we could write a letter. We are out of the habit of envelope correspondence but this is a time when it can be most appropriate.

◆ We can say exactly what we wish to say without embarrassment, taking our time and choosing our words.

◆ We can spare the person addressed the difficulty of coping

"Before he went did he say anything about a tin of paint...?"

''Had you had a row?''

"Why didn't you take away his car keys?"

"WELL AT LEAST HE WAS WELL INSURED."

"In all my 35 years as a doctor, this has happened only 3 other times."

"So what have you been doing with yourself?"

"Did she make her peace with God before she died?"

"I am so sorry. You just don't hear of anyone dying after having a baby these days."

"...and then I had to listen to his mother go on about how her cat had just died after a long illness."

"If it's any consolation, I wish my ex-husband was dead."

'I'm so sorry – we'll update our files.'

"Did he smoke?"

"So what are you going to do with his tools?"

"Life is for the living."

"The kids are young, they will most likely forget him!"

"You seem to be taking this very well."

"Don't look back."

"God has a plan for everything."

"It's no good living in the past."

"Why didn't you get him some help?"

"At least he lived a happy and successful life."

"God needed him more."

''It's time you moved on.''

"I heard you cried in church."

"At least your children are all grown up."

"Maybe it was all for the best.."

Go away!*

"I suppose you feel entirely responsible. You mustn't."

"Didn't you see the warning signs?"

"So, how do your husband's parents feel?"

"You've got to be strong now for the sake of the children."

''Don't pine your life away over a dead man.''

* ... or some similar phrase

with our difficulties.

◆ A letter is also a document that can be kept and later re-read. They are often treasured for years.

How we can help them to help us

If we are the person doing the grieving, we should be gentle with our comforters. We should try to understand their difficulty – there's very little that people can *say* or *do* to lessen the way we're feeling. Any comment or advice about how we can make ourselves 'feel better' is almost always insensitive; we are so locked into the freshness and particularities of our distress that any 'good ideas' seem irrelevant. The natural tendency for people, seeing how upset we are, is to try to get us to see things in a different light – it sometimes seems like a competition to see how well we can be cheered up.

However, these 'good reasons for us not to be upset' are also 'coincidentally' good reasons for us not to upset them: the messages that come across are often bitterly rejecting.

◆ 'You should try to put it behind you and think about the future.'   (You're boring me)

◆ 'Why don't you go away for a holiday? You'll feel much better.'   (Go away)

◆ 'It was all over so quickly: he suffered nothing.'
                                                (So that's all right then)

◆ 'The last thing she would have wanted would have been to see you so upset.'   (You're being very self-indulgent)

◆ 'I always said he should have taken more exercise.'
                            (You wouldn't be so upset if he'd listened to me)

◆ 'You're only 35 – you have your whole life ahead of you.'
                                  (You can always get another husband)

◆ 'At least he achieved his ambition in life.'
                                                (So that's all right then)

◆ 'When George's wife died he had two children under five to look after.'
                            (It was much harder for him than it is for you)

◆ 'It's awful to see you so upset.'   (You're upsetting me)

◆ 'At least you've got the children.'
                              (You don't realise how fortunate you are)

◆ 'Concentrate on the good times you had together.'

(If you close your eyes you can pretend it never happened)
◆ 'You'll find there'll be days when you just want to stay in bed.'

(I'm going to counsel you – I saw this programme on TV)
◆ 'Are you really sure you wouldn't like another piece of cake.'

(I don't know what to say but I make very good cake)

It's easy to be upset by such apparent insensitivity and harder to realise that such remarks are simply fumbling attempts to make us feel better – just as we've done to others in the past. Where can we get the strength to ignore it? At first, we simply can't; later it will be easier:

> *We can't blame anyone for walking all over us. We can only notice that we are not moving out of the way.*
> Susan Jeffers, *Thoughts of Power and Love,* 1997

> *Of all the griefs that harass the distressed*
> *Sure the most bitter is a scornful jest.*
> Samuel Johnson (1709–84)

We may be wrapped up in feelings of confusion and despair, and we can be excused for not being in control of things, but, just as others have a responsibility for supporting us, they can only do this effectively if we take some responsibility for letting them know our needs. We may not wish to impose further on the kindness of others but we have some duty to make their support easier for them by indicating how we can best be helped.

We should not underestimate the practical help people can give us – shopping, cooking, looking after pets or answering the telephone. We should avoid the temptation to refuse this sort of assistance – we may think that going to the dry cleaner's or mowing the lawn are of a ludicrously low priority at present, but keeping things running normally around us can be a comfort. To open an empty fridge, or to run out of cash because we didn't go to the bank, are the sorts of irritations which can only emphasise and darken our distress.

We should make our wishes known.

◆ 'I know you mean well, but I would just like to sit by myself until tea-time.'

◆ 'You know, far from being upset, I find it very comforting to talk about her – just hearing her name spoken is good.'

◆ 'Would you mind coming round tonight and sit with me as we watch television – I really miss him in the evenings: it's so lonely.'

◆ 'Please just hold me.'

◆ 'Could I ask you to give the bathroom a bit of a clean? – I'm so ashamed of it, but I just can't manage it.'

◆ 'Would you ring his ex-wife, she needs to know but I don't want to talk to her at the moment. Tell her she's welcome to come to the funeral.'

◆ 'You know you don't have to talk – I know how awkward it is for you – but I appreciate you just being here. Please stay for lunch.'

We may wonder, with or without reason, whether other people are observing us as victims or potential patients. Their attitude to us will be different. Are we showing 'enough' grief – or too much? There's nothing we can do about this: it may seem intrusive and meddling but it's done with the best of intentions.

Other support

It's been suggested that a reasonable formula for an effective support system is:

◆ 25 per cent self-support
◆ 20 per cent partner support
◆ 55 per cent support outside the home.

We'll be looking at how we can help *ourselves* much more than we think in Chapter 7.

If we have a concerned partner, they will normally be a key figure through the difficult times – although there may be a temptation to rely on them more than we need.

If, however, it is our partner whose death we are grieving we will need to be much more reliant on other relatives and friends for support. This may be less reliable, but, nevertheless, most people will come through unscathed.

Where we can identify no one to whom we can talk easily, and we are in some distress, it might be worth contacting an organisation like Cruse Bereavement Care (CRUSE) who will provide a welcoming environment either in a group or face to face.

Cruse Bereavement Care

Cruse Bereavement Care is the largest bereavement charity in the UK, with nearly 200 branches – there should be one in your nearest large town. It offers help from trained volunteers to bereaved people regardless of age, sex, race, religion, disability or sexual preference. It provides:

◆ a free counselling service for individuals – personal and confidential

◆ opportunities for contact with others through bereavement support groups

◆ advice and information on practical matters, backed by a wide range of publications.

Anyone can make a direct contact. The address of the head office is on page 188. You'll find your local branch in the phone book or if there isn't a local branch you can ring the UK Cruse Bereavement Line on 0870 167 1677. Where the bereaved person has consented, they will be happy to talk to a family member or a friend.

Many people may have an image of the organisation working only with older widows. It was begun in 1959 and named after the story in the Old Testament about the widow who shared her last jar of oil with the prophet Elijah – a 'cruse' is an earthenware vessel for holding oil. However, in 1986 they decided to extend their service to all bereaved people and *anyone* can be reassured that they will be welcome.

There is even a Cruse Youth Line (0808 8081 677 Monday to Friday 9.30–5pm, Saturday and Sunday 3–5pm). This is for 'anyone old enough to make a telephone call and young enough to be called youth'. You can remain anonymous if you want to – nobody else will be contacted. It can be about any loss – family, friends, teachers, even pets. This can be a useful service as it is outside a family who may be preoccupied with their own grief – or, indeed, the young person may have lost someone they would normally have talked to.

At Cruse you may not be in touch with a 'professional counsellor' but there are advantages. The volunteers will have a wide experience of bereavement and be able to provide an interested and empathetic ear. There are very good reports from people who have used Cruse.

Bereavement counselling

> *When you finally understand that you, and no one else, creates what goes on in your head, you will at last be in control of your experience of life.*
> Susan Jeffers, *Thoughts of Power and Love,* 1997

Counsellors see about 100,000 people a year – although this is probably an underestimate. The UK Register of Counsellors has 3,000 members but it's estimated that there are a further 25,000 practitioners who are unregistered.

There is no evidence that counselling 'works' – but it's not possible to research effectiveness when the material is so vague. People are either 'for' or 'against' it. Many people find counselling intrusive, impersonal and manipulative. On the other hand others find the experience challenging, objective and creative. The choice is yours: if you believe in it – it may work for you, if you don't – it won't. If you are shy of informal contacts and remain alone with your grief it might be worth considering it.

Remember that bereavement is a normal response to loss and it is unusual for us to need any professional help. The chances are that the way we are feeling will change naturally with time and our own sense of getting back to normal.

However, if you can notice no change at all for the better after a couple of months – and especially if you think that things are getting worse – you may be falling into a pattern of chronic, 'stuck' grief which may need some serious attention.

Counselling should generally be time-limited, focused on current problems and, at the beginning, it should be concerned with the 'here and now' rather than looking in depth at your personality and background. As with medication, a significant number of people (20 to 50 per cent) may drop out of counselling shortly after its initiation for various reasons.

Nearly half of GP surgeries now have counsellors attached to them, or your local Citizen's Advice Bureau may know of local resources.

It is almost impossible to be certain about a counsellor's competence in advance; there is no agreement what counselling *is* in the first place; there are hundreds of types and styles – mostly baffling to the public – and there is no national register to refer to.

The British Association for Counselling Information Service (0870 443 5252) and The UK Council for Psychotherapy (0870 167 2131) can give lists of accredited counsellors and psychotherapists who will have had at least several hundred hours of training and supervised practice.

Just what distinguishes counselling from psychotherapy remains unclear. A psychotherapist will tell you that psychotherapy is concerned with ingrained, long-standing 'damage' – she will say that counselling is more concerned with short-term immediate life crises. There's a hint that psychotherapists are more skilled and 'professional'. The best counsellors will – correctly – say that they're no different from psychotherapists in the way they approach their work. It's probably true that there is more risk of coming across an incompetent (or, more worryingly, dangerous,) counsellor – there's been a five-fold increase in their unregulated numbers since the early 1990s.

If you know of no recommended counsellor or psychotherapist, you might look in *Yellow Pages*. It's important that you are able to choose someone who will suit your needs. However, you may not be in the best shape to negotiate a suitable service and you might do better to ask someone else to make enquiries. Whoever makes these enquiries should ask some questions.

◆ Do they specialise in bereavement counselling? Many people are familiar with marital, family or personal counselling. We need to know that they have special skills in, and familiarity with, issues surrounding grief therapy.

- ◆ Our special situation needs to be explained before you even meet. Is this the sort of area where the counsellor can expect some progress?
- ◆ Do they lean towards short-term work dealing with immediate situations or are they more orientated to long-term work dealing with fundamental life situations. It is better to start with someone who will work with us for a limited number of sessions over a couple of months and who will concentrate on immediate concerns – although, obviously there may be links to the past.
- ◆ Do they work on an individual basis or with a group? We may have an opinion about this.
- ◆ If the counselling is part of medical care, will medication be involved? Although there may be a strong case for temporary anti-depressants at first, it isn't always helpful for it to continue.
- ◆ Do they inspire confidence as people?
- ◆ What are the costs involved? It may cost us upwards of £50.00 an hour.

Perhaps the easiest way to make a quick judgement is to find out how they are supervised; no serious counsellor will practice without having regular supervision themselves. During counselling itself, the only way we can tell if things are going well is through our intuition. Are we beginning to feel even a little more hopeful and positive? If, on the whole, counselling is actually making us feel worse, we may need to stop it.

There is no doubt that there are some excellent counsellors who can provide exactly what's needed – and cheap at the price – but there are also people with dubious training and experience who may disappoint us. The fact remains that the most reliable way of selecting someone is probably a recommendation from someone we know and trust.

The beginnings and endings of all human undertakings are untidy.

JOHN GALSWORTHY

CHAPTER 5

Particular Grief

S o far we've been looking at the general causes and effects of grief. There are, however, some special features of bereavement which apply to particular relationships.

The death of a partner

He that outlives a wife whom he has long loved, sees himself disjoined from the only mind that has the same hopes, and fears, and interest; from the only companion with whom he has shared much good and evil; and with whom he could set his mind at liberty, to retrace the past or anticipate the future.

Samuel Johnson (1709–84)

'She was everything to me...'

I realised that for over half my lifetime, there was no hurt or worry that had not been made better when I shared it. There had been no joy or triumph that had full meaning – been really savoured – until I had rushed home: 'I'm a genius!' and watched the quiet, amused smile that seemed to make his very spectacles glint with wry pleasure.

Mary Jones, *Secret Flowers*, 1988

When a long-term partner dies we usually lose the one person in the world who knew us best. Without them we can feel that we have become 'unknown' to the world – invisible and with a lost identity.

They were the only person to have known our secrets: our hopes and successes as well as our shortcomings and bad habits. We could choose how we presented ourselves to the rest of the world but they, uniquely, knew us fully.

When they were alive we may have been remembered for once having been young, vigorous, beautiful, sexual, or clever (maybe all five!) No one else could read our mood and needs so telepathically. If we are older adults we know how unlikely it will be for such a partnership to happen again. We may have invested our whole lifelong 'emotional savings' in the relationship and, without consultation, we are suddenly left bankrupt.

Many older people who lose their spouses will have moved into marriage at a young age directly from their childhood home. They will never have experienced what it is like to live alone and this can be a fearful experience added to their sense of loss. Younger people are more and more used to having a period of independence before settling into relationships.

'I sometimes think I'm losing my mind...'

In a sense we *do* lose a part of our mind when a partner dies after a long relationship. Over the years so much of 'who we are' has been associated with the other person – to the extent that we become lost in each other. It is only when they die that we are shocked to see how much of 'ourselves' remains and how much we were dependent on each other.

We need to discover – and reclaim – those parts of ourselves which have died with our partner before we can put ourselves back together again. And we have to do it on our own; the only person who could really have helped us is the one whose loss we are mourning.

There's work to be done

We are not the *victims* of bereavement.

Grief is not something that happens to us as we stand by, bracing ourselves against its unpredictable ravages.

The (hard) truth is that we have created our own grief. We did not want it this way, but the more of ourselves that we invested in our attachment to the person who has died, the greater will be our distress now. We may think, rightly, that the relationship was worth it – life would be a poor thing if the best that could be said was that we 'avoided pain' – but we can't avoid the bleak truth that the present suffering is of our own making.

In the same way that we are not the 'object' of grief, we cannot resume our lives by simply resting until it goes away again. We will only resolve our bereavement by working at it. This means examining all the hooks of our attachment and carefully removing them. Some of these hooks – fine fish-hooks – will be easily cut away; we'll soon be able to learn how to programme the CD player ourselves, we'll soon learn how to survive without home-made marmalade.

Some of our attachments to the person who has died, however, will be harder to move – tenacious psychological grappling-irons.

- Our social timidity may have meant that we used her confidence as a 'front' at social gatherings, allowing us to remain in the background.
- We had always felt nervous about being in the house alone when he was away on business.
- We had always been proud of the way she kept the front garden but we haven't the same interest in gardening.
- We had never learned to drive and we bought a house in the country just before he died.
- We had grown to depend entirely on her for support and affection.

The work of bereavement is first of all to identify what these hooks are and work out how we will manage to become detached from them. Doing nothing is not an option: they will not rust away of their own accord – if nothing happens they will remain forever embedded in dead memories and will anchor us, disabled, to the past.

It's a bother (and it couldn't have come at a worse time), but there's *work* to do.

It's not just a question of deciding what we're going to do now and in the future. Effective grieving involves reflecting over our past and considering how we have been changed by our (now lost) relationship.

- Am I different now than before we met? Do I want to keep this difference?
- What have I given up to sustain the relationship? Can I stop giving it up now?
- What were the good things? Were they important? Can I re-

create them some other way?

◆ Was my emotional investment worth the price I paid?

◆ What am I pleased to be rid of? How will this make a difference?

◆ What did I want my life to be like? What did I pretend it was like? What do I want it to be now?

It's important for us not to allow ourselves to be swept away in a wave of vague, generalised depression. It's really worth looking closely at these details of what our attachment was about; if we can't do it for ourselves we're either going to have to seek help from someone else for our grief or carry it about with us into the future.

I am learning to look at your life *again*
Instead of your death and departing.
Quoted by Barbara Ward in *Healing Grief,* 1993

'Thirty years of marriage and she never shed a tear!'

One of the unfortunate aspects of bereavement is that, at the very time you want to retreat from the world for a while, the world seems to want you to display your grief publicly and in an appropriate way.

There is a fascination in grief and mourning. As onlookers, it is as though we are anticipating our own future grief (maybe even imagining the grief of others at our own eventual death). There is an unconscious need to see mourning 'performed'; it's the aftermath of one of life's many dramas and, like all drama, we can learn how to behave from observing it.

Unfortunately, we tend to be insensitive in our estimation of the 'performance'. Our fairy-tale expectation is that great love will result in inconsolable weeping and if there are no outward signs of great distress we imagine a 'less than perfect' relationship. (The fact is that if there is any simple connection between the two it is likely to be the other way round – a difficult relationship is likely to cause more regretful grief than a close, open one.)

'What she needs is...'

Maybe it's a well-intentioned distraction from the pain but other people will suddenly be able to think up all sorts of 'helpful things' we can do.

- ◆ 'Throw yourself into work.'
- ◆ 'Take a couple of months off.'
- ◆ 'Go on holiday.'
- ◆ 'Try and have a good cry.'

After a while they will get around to deciding whether we should move house or get married again.

It's one of the minor drawbacks of being bereft that others will treat us like children. We can't really complain because part of us may want to be 'parented' just now and, after all, it's the way we have behaved to others in the past.

It's best to try and take some control and use this goodwill in a positive way. Work out what people *can* do for us that will be useful.

'She had a lot to put up with during the last couple of years...'

If our partner had been heavily dependent on us for their care in the time leading up to their death we may have become a person who was indispensable. We may have partly resented this and we may have become exhausted and depressed by it. It's surprising, however, how used we can become to a demanding role. When our partner dies – and this also applies to other relationships – we are suddenly faced with the added loss of this all-absorbing caring function. We are no longer 'needed'. This redundancy can give an added edge to the sharpness of early grief.

'If I could just turn the clock back ten years...'

It's easy to get stuck in the tramlines of 'if onlys'. There's something self-generating about guilt – the more we dwell on it the more exaggerated it becomes. Eventually we become trapped under a black cloud of stagnant regrets – everything in the relationship now seems to be 'our fault' and the burden seems a suitable punishment for our previous actions (or neglect). To break away from it seems too easy a release from our self-punishment, so we may unconsciously allow ourselves to become stuck in what could become a long-lasting depression.

If you genuinely wish to commit psychological and social suicide in this way you owe it to yourself to ask a few questions about your past relationship first.

◆ On the whole were you happy? Was he?
◆ Did you want to do the right thing? Did he want to do the right thing?
◆ Did you try to do the right thing? Did he try to do the right thing?
◆ Did you regret it when it went wrong? Did he regret it when it went wrong?
◆ What was your part in the failure? What was his part in the failure?
◆ What could you have done to improve things? What could he have done to improve things?
◆ Why did you fail? Why did he fail?
◆ Would you like to have tried again? Would he have liked to have tried again?
◆ If you had died first would you like to think of him suffering like you?
◆ Would he think you were right to be suffering like this?

Single again

The loss of a partner will alter the way that others perceive us. Previously we may have been seen as an active part of a cooperative partnership – part of a complete unit. Bereavement will bring a new role for us: the widow or widower.

The widow

> *He that would woo a maid must feign, lie and flatter,*
> *But he that woos a widow must down with his britches and at her.*
>
> Folk saying

There are ten times as many widows in Britain as widowers.

There's usually no shortage of people who want to give support to a bereaved man, but widows can have a harder time. No matter how independent-minded or assertive she is, other people will want to impose their widowist expectations on her – and she may be hard put to resist the pressure to conform.

In our couple-dominated social life a widow is often seen as an embarrassment. This can be so strong that she herself may feel drawn into a lonely, secluded existence as a 'victim'. Where we see this happening as outsiders we should try to discourage it because once it becomes a habit it may be with her permanently.

Fortunately, younger people are much more independent in their relationships; they are also more used, and better equipped, to deal with change. Maybe they'll also learn to deal with death more sensibly. Nowadays young women under 30 generally have equality with young men; they have the same opportunities and there are equal expectations of them.

However, this is not true of people presently of widowing age. We know about feminism and equality and we are against discrimination, but we retain a folk memory of the widow myth. In the myth, the widow, particularly if young, is a dangerous woman:

◆ she has lost a (presumably sexually active) relationship and is likely to be a prey on someone else's husband
◆ she may have a large inheritance from the marriage, which enhances her attraction and power.

Widows are 'dangerous' because they have become 'free' of the 'control' of their dead husband: they threaten the stability of the old-fashioned traditional male-dominated system.

This will thankfully not be the case for our grandchildren, but that is no consolation to the lonely present-day 'ex-partner' (let's look for another word). She may feel a social coolness towards her and she may feel particularly vulnerable over her new status.

A good occasion for courtship is when the widow returns from the funeral.

Jacula Prudentium

This vulnerability is sharpened by what may be a strong

impulse to jump into a new relationship as soon as possible often for no other reason than to fill the gap left by the death.

The loss of a sexual partner may also cause someone to seek casual, impersonal sex as a purely physical comfort. The resulting complications – and the criticism of others – can make things worse, so be careful.

Writing in the *International Journal of Psychoanalysis* (17 June 1994) about Agutainos widows in British Columbia, A. Cochrane wrote:

> *She may only go out at an hour when she is unlikely to meet anyone, for whoever sees her is thought to die a sudden death. To prevent this she knocks with a wooden peg on the trees as she goes along warning people of her presence. It is believed that the very trees on which she knocks will soon die.*
>
> 'A Little Widow is a Dangerous Thing.'

And a final sobering thought:

> *Three out of four women, presently in marriages which don't end in divorce, will become widows one day.*
>
> Paul Gebhard

The widower

Maybe because he may show his grief less and seem more self-sufficient and powerful, a widower may seem to need less emotional support than a widow. This is often a shame because many widowers are hit harder than widows. Often they lack the close friendships that women enjoy and are often socially stranded. They may have been totally reliant on their partners for all their emotional support.

It may be that we should tentatively set aside a widower's protestations that he wants to be left alone and make sure that he knows that we are available if he wants help.

The younger widowed father may receive more neighbourly and family attention and support – he may be assumed to need help with child care. However, he may be aware of a new sexual availability he has which may attract unwelcome attention.

Same-sex partner grief

Although people may not approve of the expectations of others about how they should grieve, there are, at least, some clear guidelines about the role of someone who has lost a spouse. There is some comfort from being able to take refuge in the ready-made roles of a widow or widower. People in same-sex relationships mostly have to make it up as they go along. There is no common concept of gay grief and there are no role models for gay widowhood.

Is bereavement exactly the same as for people in opposite-gender relationships? There's no reason why it shouldn't be – it's just that everything that's been written has been in the context of conventional marriage relationships.

There are, however, some clear differences about how others respond to the loss of someone in a same-sex partnership.

◆ How publicly known was the relationship? Many gay people may not have declared themselves as such; if their relationship is not acknowledged there may be an important lack of support for the grieving partner. What's more, they may meet up with scorn, ridicule or rejection.

◆ Even if they are 'out', kindly disposed straight friends and colleagues may not appreciate the extent of their loss – many people assume that same-sex relationships are less 'serious' than straight partnerships: there may, for example, be a careless lack of encouragement to take time off work.

◆ Not only may there be a lack of positive support but the surviving partner may be carelessly (or brutally) ignored by other grieving family members who move in and 'take over'. They may be excluded from planning or attending the funeral.

Although HIV/AIDS is not currently an issue particular to gay people, it used to be. People who have been in long partnerships may well have had several friends who have died or who are HIV positive. The effects of multi-bereavements can be severe – there isn't enough space to mourn a death before others happen; feelings become jumbled and confused.

In conventional marriages the main carer of someone who has died – usually the spouse – would normally have the principal role in decision-making, consents, funeral arrangements and executing a will. Their right as next of kin and beneficiary are established even if there is no will.

Same-sex partners, however, have no legal status. If they were financially dependent on the deceased they could make a claim if there was no will, but they otherwise have no rights.

This makes it essential that both partners have drawn up their own wills making their wishes clear. There should also be agreement by everyone about funeral arrangements – who will organise it and who will attend.

The greatest need for many homosexual men and women is to be able to find support – not necessarily psychotherapy or counselling, but someone or a group that can be openly and positively available to them to use as they wish. Increasingly there are support groups available for surviving partners of people who had AIDS but there is less support available where AIDS was not a factor.

Bereaved same-sex partners are more depressed, they consider suicide more frequently and they tend to make more frequent use of help from medical, psychological and spiritual professionals than those widowed in conventional relationships. You can find further information from Cruse Bereavement Care; the Lesbian and Gay Bereavement Project; The Terrence Higgins Trust or The National AIDS Helpline (addresses and telephone numbers are on pages 188–90).

The death of parents

> *One reason you are stricken when your parents die is that the audience you've been aiming at all your life – shocking it, pleasing it – has suddenly left the theatre.*
>
> Katherine Whitehorn, the *Observer*, 1983

We have the greatest opportunity and the longest time to prepare for the deaths of our parents.

More than anyone they are usually the people we expect to die before us. From an early age we will unconsciously have imagined what it will be like for us to be alone in the world. It sounds an overstatement for someone in middle age, successful and worldly wise, to have an anxiety about coping without their parents. However, we all have an unconscious emotional dependency on them – dramatically created in early childhood when we were most vulnerable to possible abandonment.

When they die this long-forgotten infant fear of desertion is triggered and we may not understand why we suddenly feel so strangely vulnerable and depressed.

We also didn't realise how much we have depended on them throughout our lives. We may rarely see them but they will usually have stood in the background as the main authentic, unselfish provider of love; we could always depend on this whether we deserved it or not. They were the people who were always interested in what we were doing.

We are the product of their genes and one of our main aims in life will have been to demonstrate what good use we have made of their genetic material.

And yet this most important of relationships is so often taken for granted – because it has been the most complex and difficult to describe. All sorts of resentments, jealousies and rivalries are mingled with love, comfort and protection. In our emotional filing cabinet our parents have by far the thickest file.

This is also the relationship that we are most likely to have neglected because we've never had to work at it to keep it going. The shock of loss will usually bring home to us how central our parents have been in making us who we are – and almost inevitably – how little appreciation we have shown.

If we've had a difficult relationship with them, we are likely to have cut ourselves off from them. Their death in these circumstances will be hard for us to take. There will be the remorse that we didn't make our peace but there will be another sense of loss. Bob Monkhouse wrote about the death of his mother:

> *I collapsed with sorrow and loss, grieving not so much for her death as for her life – racked with regret for the lack of all that could and should have existed between us.*
>
> Crying with Laughter, Century 1993

On the other hand if we've never been very emotionally involved with them we needn't necessarily have any regrets. Jonathan Miller had a cool, distant relationship with his father;

there was a distinct lack of attachment. In a voice showing no sign of resentment or guilt he told Anthony Clare: 'I didn't miss him at all when he died.' ('In the Psychiatrist's Chair', Radio 4, September 1999.)

If we're grown up when they die we're not likely to get the support from others that we need – after all they've been taking their parents for granted too.

Losing a parent when you're a child

> *Sixteen years a maiden*
> *One twelve-month a Wife,*
> *One half hour a Mother,*
> *And then I lost my Life.*

Epitaph: Folkestone

It's true to say that the main business of childhood – growing up – should have little concern with death. However, our attitudes to death and dying will have a subtle, but important, influence in shaping those of our children. If we have a healthy acceptance of mortality they will have fewer problems: if, as most us do, we find it hard to face our own death, it will be inevitable that our children will develop the same confusion. 'Don't be morbid!' is a learned attitude, not a genetically inherited one.

This is not to say that we should dwell on the precariousness of life and the imminence of death. We do have a responsibility, however, of being clear with our children that death is a normal, natural and inevitable part of life. Adults are able to spread their emotional investments across many people – friends, partners, children, lovers. Children have everything invested in their parents. They are short of resources in other ways too:

◆ the whole concept of death is unknown territory
◆ they have only a muddled vocabulary for expressing feelings
◆ they have not come upon grief before and don't know that the pain will diminish in time
◆ they can't be independent and find it hard to become emotionally dependent on someone else.

As they develop, the reality of the death comes into focus and the new information may bring its own grief. Hope Edelman in *Motherless Daughters* (Hodder & Stoughton 1994) describes one situation where a 4-year-old had been told that her mother had died in her sleep because of petrol fumes. It didn't occur to her until she was 20 that it had been suicide by carbon monoxide poisoning; she then had to go through a new cycle of recurrent grieving.

Young children fare badly when the surviving parent:
◆ has a slow recovery
◆ is exceptionally depressed
◆ appears totally unaffected
◆ becomes tired and disorganised.

The baby's response to a parent's death

If another major carer continues with her care she will be unlikely to experience any great sense of loss if a parent dies.

By the age of six to eight months, however, she will have become bonded with her mother or carer and will be unsettled with strangers. From then on if that carer disappears she will grieve for their loss: this may show itself in lack of interest in food, whimpering and apparent withdrawal. A child of this age will retain no conscious long-term memory of a lost parent.

Toddlers

Toddlers, are sensitive to the mood of the home and may need a lot of warm, reassuring cuddles. Explanations about death will be useless – but it's wise to watch what we say: 'gone to sleep', 'gone away' and 'gone to heaven' are too fanciful and open to all sorts of mistaken conclusions. It's best to be factual and accurate about what has happened. Later the toddler will come across the concept of death and will begin to grapple with its meaning.

We can help children by – tentatively – putting clear words to their feelings. They won't yet have learned to understand the loss – so any hurt is likely to be directly and strongly expressed. We should listen for the 'message' behind the words.

They also have a crude sense of morality and may think that

the death was caused by 'badness' – they know that sometimes they, too, are 'bad'... so ...

The best way to explain someone's death is to do it in very concrete terms – '...and he became so ill that his heart stopped working and he died: he will not be alive ever again, even though we are all very sad.' Although it sounds simplified – even brutal – at this age the *physical* truth about death is clearer than the use of concepts of religion, responsibility or blame.

At this age feelings are often expressed through play and we may be able to allow a child to talk about how they feel or to give reassurance by becoming involved in their play activities.

The older child

By the age of 7 the growing child will be less focused on himself and more interested in the rest of the world. The 'awful truth' about the inevitability of dying and the possibility of his own death will take a hold. He will also begin to be able to imagine what it would be like if his parents died (at a time when he is so dependent on them).

His mind may dwell gruesomely on what happens to the body after death or what fears there might be in an imagined afterlife. This could all be complicated if he has concepts of 'naughtiness', guilt or blame.

Our first thought may be to protect a young child from the pain of grief and we may mistakenly try to play down the distress of bereavement. We are also likely, unfortunately, to be in no fit state ourselves to be able to give attention to other people's needs. The result may be that feelings of loss and confusion in children are overlooked. This may be an occasion when someone other than the surviving parent could take a special interest in the children.

Children should generally be fully involved with the funeral and, far from needing protection, they need to be able to talk about their fears, anxieties and questions.

It's sometimes hard for us really to believe it, but *honest* expression of feelings is *always* positive:

A child can live through anything so long as he or she is told

*the truth and is allowed to share with loved ones the natural
feelings people have when they are suffering.*

Eda le Shan

We should not be surprised if children often 'leave off'
apparent grieving for periods of time – behaving as if nothing
has happened. This can seem heartless and unnerving, but it is
as though the grief was too intense to sustain and 'short rests'
are required.

The older child's experience

By the time of puberty a child will have a clear idea of death.
However this will remain theoretical and untroubling unless
she actually experiences the loss of someone close. This will
bring home the reality of mortality and may be frightening. She
may only get to grips with the loss six to nine months after the
death when the surviving parent is beginning to recover the
strength to feel better. It is as though the child puts things on
hold until they can be assured of positive attention to their
emotional needs.

If we lose a parent before we're ten there is a markedly
increased tendency towards depression, low self-esteem and
emotional breakdown later in life.

*Some people think that children are too young to understand
about death. Sadly they are not too young to misunderstand.*
Virginia Ironside, *You'll Get Over It!*, 1996

Adolescents

Losing a parent in our early teens is especially hard. The whole
point of adolescence is to develop physical, and emotional
independence from our parents; there's a lot of dressing up and
play-acting involved but the teenager's task is to ditch
childhood and its ignorance, impotence and dependence and
get down to being a self-sufficient, worldly-wise grown up. The
truth, of course, is that both parents and child secretly know
the rules of the deadly serious game and conspire to keep good
faith.

When a parent dies in these circumstances it is an

strength and resilience, which may hide much of their loss.

Indeed, far from receiving sensitive care, others may look to them to give support. They may be called on to take responsibilities for which they are not ready – arranging the funeral, dealing with the estate, disposing of possessions. They may be seen as the natural 'comforter' of the surviving parent or they may be pushed into a substitute parental role towards younger brothers and sisters.

Young adulthood is a time for establishing ourselves in a job and learning how to live in a long-term relationship. There is a powerful need to project an image of positive competence, optimism and strength. Our investment in these aspects of our lives may mean that we 'postpone' our grieving needs for the more pressing needs of others.

The result is that there are thousands of older adults showing signs of chronic, unexplained depression, which can be linked to inadequate attention to their personal need for grieving many years earlier.

There's also the regret – the anger even – that the dead parent will never see the promising future we have in store for ourselves; our children will never know their grandparent. There may even be an unconscious, lingering, 'little-boy-lost' feeling of abandonment – even though we're 63 years old.

We may also have been denied an 'adult–adult' friendship with them as we grow out of the complications of the parent–child relationship.

The time following a parent's death is often a time when we gain a fuller picture of them. We may meet distant relatives and friends who may throw a new light on their personality and their past. Their completed life will now be 'whole'. For the first time we may be able to look back and reflect on life in general – 'Was that all . . .?' We may become interested in researching family history as we take on our new role of 'descendant'.

While our parents lived, we never quite escaped from defining ourselves as 'somebody's child'. Now we switch to being 'somebody's mother' or 'somebody's brother' or, for someone without relatives, alone in the world.

If you are pregnant when a parent dies it is likely that your normal grief reactions will be affected. Your body knows its priorities and it won't allow you to shift your focus and emotional attention from the new baby. It may not be until after the birth that your bereavement hits you. This can then be a bleak, depressing time, for not only are you mourning your loss but you are aware that your parent never saw their grandchild – all this when you should have been benefiting from their physical and emotional support as you adjust to your new role. This can be a strong underlying cause of post-natal depression.

In one study (Jacobson and Ryder 1979) it was found that 20 per cent of older women who lost their mother found that they became unable to enjoy their sexuality. They also found that it's not uncommon for some men to 'retreat into childish and effeminate activities' following the death of their father.

Being in a long-term relationship will provide a massive support to us when a parent dies. Being a carefree bachelor may have its advantages, but, among single men who commit suicide, an amazing 60 per cent have been found to have lost their mother in the previous three years (only 6 per cent of the general single male population will have had a similar loss.)

Often a mother is the 'mediator' or 'communicator' in family relationships; she may be the one who has always encouraged discussion of feelings or calmed down conflicts. When she dies a vital component of the whole family may die and things may never be the same again. Who'll ever remember your sister's wedding anniversary now?

Although the death of both parents can bring feelings of loneliness and abandonment that can turn us in on ourselves, it can also be the jump-start for us to move on in our personal development. For the first time we are free of some of the restraints on our feelings and behaviour inherited from our childhood: through the loss and abandonment we can emerge to positive independence for the first time.

Family grief

> June was 14 when she died. I was five years younger but we'd never been very close as sisters. She was definitely my mother's favourite. When she got leukaemia that was it: everything

revolved around her. It was 'June this...' and 'June that...'.
Mum devoted her life to her. I was sorry for Dad – he had to
do everything.

We had to cancel a holiday because 'June has a hospital
appointment'. There was a collection for us all to go to
Disneyland but in the end there was only enough to pay for
Mum and her. It's a terrible thing when you come to hate
your sister. Imagine how I felt when she died. But it's Mum I
blame. Things have never been the same since – that's 40
years. It's as though she takes a pleasure in rubbing it in –
'Just think, our June would have been 54 next week'.

Nancy Gail

So far we've been considering the way that a death can affect
individuals – we're suddenly forced to adjust to who we're
going to be in a world without the dead person. In many ways
this is a straightforward task compared to the work that a
family may have do when they lose a key member – and in
families *everyone* is a vital component.

A personal relationship is two-dimensional and there is
some clarity about roles and functions. It may be painful but
we can usually, at least, understand what we have lost and,
eventually, what we need to do to resolve our grief.

A family, however, is a more complicated matter.

Families grow silently over the years, each member
establishing a role for themselves – or having one assigned;
sometimes it's not clear. but in any case, we all know our
place:

A solves the problems	B is the clever one
C has the bright ideas	D needs all the sympathy
E makes the decisions	F is the one who gets the blame
G is in charge	H cleans out the goldfish.

Usually, if all goes well a family will be open and positive,
aiming at good relationships and personal growth. More likely
– and this happens in most families – roles and expectations
will not be so clear. There may be unspoken
misunderstandings, rivalries and secrets which may (or may
not) be very serious and which pass unnoticed because we
conspire to keep things on an even keel.

When someone dies this long-preserved equilibrium is destroyed. Each family member will have their own special grief, which may not be understood by the others. They will all be thrown together, their attitudes and behaviour may be confused and skewed. This becomes fertile ground for tension, recrimination, accusations, demands and hurtful remarks.

In a study by Ira O. Glick in 1974, 28 per cent of widows reported having angry feelings towards family members – officiousness, meddling, not doing enough. The main target was their own 'interfering' mothers – maybe because their present vulnerability evoked past dependency. Sisters came out best (for men *and* women): brothers and brothers-in-law weren't much help at all. In the same study 42 per cent of these same widows expressed dissatisfaction with women in their *partner's* family.

There'll be a lot of – usually unexpressed – thinking going on:

- Who organises and pays for the funeral?
- What's in the will?
- Who's to 'blame' for the death?
- Who's grieving most/too much/not enough?
- Who's being inconsiderate and insensitive?
- Why won't they stop telling me what to do?
- Now that my partner's dead what is my relationship with her family?
- With mother gone who will be on my side in the future?
- Who'll keep father from drinking too much now that my brother's been killed?
- She wouldn't be so upset if it was me that had died.
- Would I be so upset if it was her that had died?

We must guard against family collusion in creating substitute roles for bereaved young people; it is easy for a boy to become 'the man of the house' or for his sister to become 'a little mother'. This is dangerous because it denies their own needs for development. One widow, Jackie, talked on Radio 4 (*Home Truths*, May 1999) about how her 7-year-old son would ask her if she had remembered her keys when she went out; on another occasion when she was talking about hiring a car he asked, 'What about the insurance?' She regretted that he had taken on the burden of such concerns.

However, in spite of all these problems there is a brighter side. It is common for a death to bring family members into a new closeness and the time around the funeral may gather together far-flung relatives who rarely meet. Grieving people also commonly turn towards their family for support; one study reported that 40 per cent of bereaved spouses named a family member as the person who had been most helpful to them.

A child loses a brother or sister

Unless a brother or sister has given substantial care to a very young child, he will not be seriously bereaved if they die. Under the age of about three months a baby has little memory of any family members when they are out of sight, so long as there is one major caretaker.

As the child gets older he will know what death is – but maybe only in the same way that he responds to the death of a pet. The importance of relationships within our families usually only becomes really evident as we get older – although there are often close sibling relationships at this age, which may need to be mourned. Nonetheless, a young child's apparent detachment or callous indifference may be unnerving to the rest of the family:

After the funeral can I have his bedroom?

Young children usually think the world revolves around them and gradually come to realise how powerful they can be; it's possible they may feel that somehow they are responsible for wishing a brother dead – there can be confusion between feelings, acts, guilt and responsibility. Because young children don't have the vocabulary to express subtle feelings their grief may show itself in unusual behaviour.

All parents will make big mistakes coping with the grief of their other children after the death of a child. We will have temporarily lost our normal sensitivity to their needs. We'll know that it's an important loss for them and we will stumble to try to do our best to prevent them being hurt.

The child may collude with us to avoid dealing with things by being quiet and withdrawn; we might fool ourselves that they're not taking it too badly. However, they may be suffering much more than we are – they haven't the experience to see the context and know what the future might be. So we need to do something. The danger is that we'll try to think up complicated things to do and say in our well-intentioned effort to do 'the right thing'.

The best thing to do is to respond openly and authentically – giving as much attention and physical contact as we are able. There is no need to justify, soothe or protect their feelings. The key is honesty – about what has happened, how everyone is feeling and the future security of family life.

It's usually not helpful to be negative, but we may need to steel ourselves to resist going down unhelpful cul-de-sacs. So, here are some 'don'ts'.

◆ Don't try to minimise his reactions or protect him from his feelings. Allow him to be part of the family sadness.

◆ On the other hand, don't put pressure on the child to express his feelings; he may do it more through his behaviour than with words. He may be able to handle his grief only in short snatches. Let him be in charge of the pace of his own grief.

◆ Don't expect his response to be the same as ours.

◆ We won't be able to hide our own feelings – we shouldn't even try. Our own tears give the child permission to show real feelings too.

◆ If there are no tears we shouldn't assume he's not grieving.

◆ Don't try to simplify things – 'She's gone to Heaven and will be happier now'; 'You'll feel better in a few weeks'. It's OK to say that we 'don't know'.

◆ Don't make demands on him to give you comfort.

◆ Don't use woolly language: 'Mary died' not 'Mary passed away'.

◆ Don't single him out for special treatment. He may need the comfort of the structure and limits of his day-to-day life.

Although young children should be given the opportunity to talk about their feelings we should be careful about pushing them into confronting their loss. It's easy to be over-enthusiastic about 'helping them to face up to the situation'.

Dr Richard Harrington of the Department of Child and Adolescent Psychiatry of the Royal Manchester Children's Hospital challenged (in May 1999) the idea that bereavement counselling should be offered to children:

> *This assumption is unwise. There are plenty of examples in child mental health of interventions that were thought at first to be beneficial but proved in randomised trials to be harmful.*
>
> *We cannot be confident that the theory behind some childhood bereavement programmes is sound. It may not be necessary to encourage children through the painful process of crying and expressing sadness. Such procedures could be harmful.*
>
> *Failure to mourn (in children) does not seem to be linked to later psychological disorders.*

Dr Harrington claims that most bereaved children do not develop serious psychiatric problems later in life. It needs a certain maturity and developed thinking capacity to become depressed and children normally have a natural protective resilience to see them through the crisis – much more so than adolescents and adults. To insist on invading this self-defence can do more harm than good.

As time goes by parents need to be aware – where a sibling has died – that remaining children are protected from feelings spilling over from the dead child. We may become overprotective and frightened of normal risks for fear of losing another child; we may put the dead child 'on a pedestal' and measure the others against their 'perfection'. They may feel that they have to replace or 'make up for' their dead brother.

Regrets about simmering sibling rivalries from early childhood may cause a child to feel guilty about the death of a brother or sister.

The natural egotism of adolescence will assume that no one feels grief quite so sharply as they do. (In fact bereavement may well be their most intense emotional experience to date.) Their aspiration towards 'responsible' adulthood, however, may prevent a young person from showing 'childish' emotions. In this way they may appear 'strong' and become a 'crutch' for someone else's grief.

The important thing is for us to *include* our children in our own bereavements; to show by the way that we express ourselves that talking about our loss is a mature, healthy thing to do. On the other hand it may be that they will prefer to seek emotional support from their friends rather than their family.

When our own child dies...

> *By the calamity of April last, I lost my little all in the world; and have no soul left who can make any corner of this world into a home for me any more. Bright, heroic, tender, true and noble was that lost treasure of my heart, who faithfully accompanied me in all the rocky ways and climbing, and I am forever poor without her.*
>
> <div align="right">Thomas Carlyle (1795–1881), <i>Letters</i></div>

Just as we expect our parents to die before us so we, like our parents, invest our hopes and support in our children. It was our parents' job to pass on their genes to us and our basic biological purpose is to create new gene combinations for future generations: there is no other biological purpose in life. If we have a child who dies we *could* honestly say – without the emotional exaggeration that usually accompanies it – 'There is no reason for me to go on living.'

However, there are more aspects to our life than simple genetic regeneration and we can eventually find many good reasons to go on. However, this initial real sense of meaninglessness is what sets the death of a child apart from all others. Compared to the loss of a son or daughter our grief at other deaths seems an indulgence; here we are up against the ultimate loss.

Other people, apart from our parents, usually came into our affections by accident – we chose to become attached and, although their deaths may be devastating, we can in time adjust to life without them. Children, however, are special – we generated them from our flesh and we usually have an invariable commitment to supporting their growth and development as long as we live. This is a commitment which, once started, cannot be stopped. When our child dies we cannot, as with other deaths, eventually accept the world without them – for us they will always exist.

We cannot accept that their hopes and potential can be stopped. We shall carry their dead memory for the rest of our lives.

When an older person dies there is normal personal grieving but, after the initial shock of the loss of a child, our first response is to challenge the circumstances – such is the 'unnatural', incredible impact of the event.

With other deaths we tend to turn our grief in on ourselves and it burns inside. Child death is different. Parents' grief is often passionately energised and turned outwards to the world in which their child has been lost. They will be driven to find out the precise cause of the death with the thought in the back of their minds that 'It won't happen again to someone else'. It may be the occasion for beginning a campaign for a change in legislation 'so that, at least, something good can come out of this . . .'

It is as though there is a need to 'achieve' something on behalf of the child – almost to make up for the child's lost achievements. Parents seem to absorb some of their child's unlived life such is the commitment and energy they will reveal. With their child gone 'nothing matters any more'; they may lose their normal reticence and become provocative and 'dangerous'.

In the short term, this 'busyness' can be helpful as an anaesthetic for the intolerable pain inside and it can mask some of the quieter feelings of bereavement, but these will surely come – the depression, the guilt, the 'if onlys'. We may begin to measure up our partner – looking for blame. It is estimated that between 70 per cent and 90 per cent of marriages where a child has died become seriously endangered or end in separation or divorce.

When an adult dies we grieve for their past life. Parents of a young child will grieve for what they have lost but they will also grieve for what the future promised. At least with an adult their past life was real – it is much harder to contemplate aspirations, unfulfilled hopes and an imagined future. In a sense the child will continue to live and grow in the parents' imagination; its presence may be so real as to cause confusion:

The thing I most fear is when some stranger innocently asks

*you how many children we have. Should I be honest and say
'two'? Susan is still so alive for me it always seems like a
betrayal. I'll always have* three *children.'*

Margaret Collinson

When we grieve for an adult we can conceive of eventual
normality – 'it's been sad, but that's life'. After the loss of a
child, however, part of us will have been permanently harmed.
We'll learn to live with the wound, but it will never heal.

*Grief fills the room up of my absent child,
Lies in his bed, walks up and down with me;
Puts in his pretty looks, repeats his words,
Remembers me of all his gracious parts;
Stuffs out his vacant garments with his form.*

Shakespeare, *King John*

Baby death

*Here lyes ye body
Of Mrs Mary Briant
Wife of Mr Thomas
Briant who dyed
November the 30th
1724 aged 39 yeares
& in har arms doth
Lye ye corps of two
Lovely babes born
Of har 8 days before
Har death one a son
Nathaniel dyed ye day
Before har a daughtr
Named Hannah dyed a few ours after har*

The May Briant and children stone, Mass. 1724

Even a very young child will have had a characteristic
personality – a presence and individuality that was evident to
family and friends and whose loss can therefore be shared.

The miscarried, recently born or stillborn child, however,
will have a socially 'unknown' identity and will not have
'existed' so tangibly for others as for the parents – especially

the mother. The parents themselves will have nothing to 'remember' about its unlived life.

Stillbirth

> *A lily of a day*
> *Is fairer in May*
> *Although it fall and die that night*
> *It was the plant and flower of light.*
>
> Ben Jonson (1573–1637)

Until recently it was assumed that a parent's bonding with their baby began only after it was born. It has now been found that this is not so. Bonding is a process that emerges much earlier, as the mother becomes aware of her pregnancy; it strengthens as the baby makes its physical presence known by her increased size and its movements within her. Ultrasound scanning puts a physical shape to the bond; by the time the baby is born mothers are commonly able to have ideas about the baby's temperament. They – and fathers to a lesser extent – already have a strong sense of attachment to their child before they have even seen it.

Research has shown that, often, parents of lost newborn babies grieve less successfully than those of older children.

Often the mother is young – without the maturity to come to terms with loss; this may be her first experience of death and her need to grieve may not be fully acknowledged. The father may be totally ignored and be less willing to talk about his feelings.

Childbirth is to do with health, growth and hope so a baby's death is always shocking, particularly if the mother's antenatal care had suggested no problem.

Because of the medical risks surrounding pregnancy and birth, parents are more ready to search for reasons for the death. They will wonder about the treatment they have had and will inevitably question their own responsibility and medical fitness for bearing children in the future.

Although the baby has no 'history' to grieve for, the parents will have constructed a fantasy reality for the child which will be made up of expectations, hopes and aspirations. They will also have thought themselves into the role of mother and father. They will have made plans, accepted new responsibilities and prepared a new lifestyle. The last months will have been a countdown to a new future. There is already so much to be lost – and bereaved.

A unique feature of baby bereavement is that its sharpness is usually limited to the parents. Friends and other family members will have their own special sense of loss, but only the mother and father will have made such a massive emotional investment. In other bereavements there will be understanding and support from people who also knew the dead person but few others will realise how great an impact the loss will have had on the dead baby's parents.

To some extent the mother's partner may also fail to understand the depth of her biological and emotional needs. She had such an intimate physical relationship with the baby and her hormone balance is poorly suited to coping with the stress of the loss. This may leave the mother unsupported and isolated.

If it is known that the baby has died in the womb, it is common for the mother to deny it or, more usually, to develop revulsion for her body – 'a living coffin'. There usually remains an irrational vestige of hope that the baby could be alive (even amongst hospital staff). This might mean that the grieving process is put 'on hold' until the dead baby is born.

The hospital will offer to arrange and provide a simple funeral free of charge. Many parents are distressed and agree to this without considering that taking their own responsibility for arranging the funeral will give some reality to their loss.

It helps also to give the baby a name. This may not seem important at the time but in the years to come the name will help focus memories.

If a baby is stillborn (born dead after the 24th week of pregnancy) the death will need to be registered in the normal way – you can ask to have a first name entered for a stillborn baby.

Miscarriage

A study in 1990 (Bansen and Stevens) estimated that clinically recognised miscarriages occur in an amazing 31 per cent of pregnancies. Because of this frequency, the non-visibility of the foetus and the assumption that there is no parent/child relationship the effects are underestimated.

Miscarriages happen usually in the early weeks and months of pregnancy – often before the pregnancy has been announced. The first sign will usually be heavy bleeding which may carry away the small foetus. The mother may not even have seen it and few people may know about it – miscarriage is, therefore, often the most private and unacknowledged of losses.

The mother will have been admitted to hospital for the 'products of conception' – as the foetus is cruelly called – to be removed and will be quickly discharged. Everything happens so quickly – yesterday there was a baby, today there isn't.

There is more awareness nowadays of the emotional needs of miscarrying mothers but they remain the most neglected and misunderstood of bereaved people.

Common sense (that most unreliable of friends) tells us that a miscarriage a few months into pregnancy is not such a great loss: the pregnancy is not visible, the mother can't feel the baby's presence – our friends will even tell us that 'perhaps it's for the best: it's nature's way'. However, a surprising study published in 1980 by Peppers and Knapp, in *Psychiatry*, showed that there was little difference in the bereavement needs of mothers who had miscarried and those who had stillborn babies or those whose babies died at birth. These mothers needed many months' grieving to recover from the loss.

In her book *Loss and Bereavement in Childbearing* (Blackwell 1994) Rosemary Mander describes a study by Bansen and Stevens in 1992:

> *These researchers found profound guilt, anger at their bodies and fear for future childbearing... The mothers' grief was long lasting; resolution of their grief may have been impeded by the sudden onset of their miscarriage, precluding any opportunities for anticipatory grieving. Social support was unforthcoming, which was compounded by unhelpful comments denigrating the loss.*

There are two organisations who can help: the Miscarriage

Association and the Stillbirth and Neonatal Death Society (see page 189).

Terminations of pregnancy

There are two sorts of terminations of pregnancy. Mostly (80 per cent) these are to do with social circumstances or the mother's health. Although it is sought by her, she will not have been able to have prevented natural hormonal preparation for the birth which will have set in an unconscious psychological anticipation whether she likes it or not. There will need therefore to be some adjustment to the loss in even the most 'straightforward' circumstances. Most women underestimate their need to grieve following a termination.

More complex still are those terminations following diagnosis of a foetal abnormality.

Because it is an unviable foetus that is aborted, unseen, and because it is with the consent of the mother there is little public acknowledgement of her grief (even less for the father's).

Far from the relief that friends might expect, the parents' emotions will be complex.

◆ Because the foetus is not seen, the 'reality' of the loss is not established. The loss does not have the 'official' recognition of death registration or funeral.

◆ This was a 'wanted' pregnancy, however abnormal; there is likely to be a strong sense of loss as well as guilt feelings. Would a 'good' mother not want to keep her baby whatever disability it might have?

◆ Because these terminations often take place later – when the pregnancy may be visible – other people may know of the decision and may be critical.

◆ Will she ever produce a 'normal' baby? Will she ever be pregnant again? – especially if she is an older woman.

In a 1989 study of 36 women who had had terminations because of foetal abnormality, three-quarters reported a severe grief reaction and a fifth needed psychiatric treatment – particularly if the operation was very late in the pregnancy or if the abnormality had been non life-threatening. The voluntary nature of the decision – far from making things easier – made them worse. (Only 5 per cent of women who had terminations for 'social' reasons reported severe grief reactions.)

Sudden Infant Death Syndrome: cot death

Although we tend to think that cot death is a modern phenomenon, the number of these apparently inexplicable baby deaths – usually up to six months of age – has remained steady over the years. The apparent increase simply reflects the dramatic decrease of all other infant deaths during the last half of the twentieth century.

A cot death sets the scene for a combination of particularly cruel circumstances.

- ◆ It happens at the height of the 'bonding' honeymoon period when the child is particularly appealing and when the parents are feeling proud and successful.
- ◆ It usually happens after the baby returns home from hospital. The parents are often inexperienced in baby care and their first instinct is to blame themselves or feel guilty about some imagined neglect.
- ◆ The usual lack of obvious explanation for the death may involve an investigation by the coroner, an inquest and questions from the police.
- ◆ There will be doubts in the minds of others about the full explanation for the death.
- ◆ Parents may be reticent about sharing their complex feelings with other people and there may be recriminations within their relationship, which may have serious long-term effects.
- ◆ Parents can be so harmed that they may withdraw from older children for fear of losing them.

If we find ourselves in such heartbreaking circumstances, we should find the strength to seek reassurance about the medical causes and the extent of our own responsibility.

Contacting groups of other parents who have been through a cot death is particularly useful. These will be able to offer individual counselling, information and local group support. You may find it helpful to join one of the local groups in raising funds for further medical research. Contact The

Foundation for the Study of Infant Deaths or SANDS, The Stillbirth and Neonatal Death Society (see page 189).

The needs of baby-bereft parents

The first requirement is for the parents to experience the reality of what has happened. It's helpful for the mother of a stillborn child to be encouraged to be fully conscious during labour, to experience labour contractions and to take part in the washing, dressing and laying-out of the baby.

There should be prompt, honest information from doctors and nurses. Often mothers have fantasies about their blame for the death – 'If only I'd rested more/smoked less/eaten better/ drunk less alcohol.' Medical information can give reassurance. The prospects for future pregnancies should also be spelled out: there will be an immediate anxiety that 'If it happened once, it'll happen again.'

It is now firmly established that it is most important for the baby to be seen and held. In a study of 22 mothers, 12 had seen their babies – all were pleased they had; 10 chose not to see their babies – all regretted it. Parents may be discouraged from having contact if the child is disfigured but *not* to see the child is to substitute fantasy images perhaps even more disturbing – forever more.

Taking photographs will give a focus and establish memories for the years to come.

Above all the grieving parents need to talk about their feelings. However, they will have trouble finding the words because it will be hard to disentangle all the facts, dreams, guilt, aspirations, regrets, fears and miseries. It may be even harder to find someone who will understand this profound need so it's important to take seriously anyone who offers an ear.

Infertility

A brief word is needed about grief and infertility. How can we grieve for a person who has never existed?

Many people who are unable to have a baby may have

spent years with their partner imagining how life would be different if they had a child; the prospect of parenthood is a very real, ever-present reality. The gradual fear that this may be impossible may cause a profound bereavement for the loss of their *expectations*.

Not only will there be grief for the loss of hope for the child they will never have – there may also be grief for their lost sense of themselves becoming a family. This is often a testing time for their relationship and the strain may cause it to break down.

If we find ourselves in this situation we won't find the same support that other bereaved people can expect. It may even be that people – not knowing the truth – will think we don't like children or that we are selfish.

The grief of grandparents

An important factor in a parent's grief is the loss of genetic inheritance to the family. This is just as true for the grandparents – our wish for our genes to be inherited doesn't stop just with our children.

The grief of grandparents, however, often remains under-recognised. The dead child's parents are the rightful focus for any support – indeed the grandparents may feel impelled to set their own feelings aside to look after their bereaved children.

Grandparents often see it as an important role of theirs to be a special support to their grandchildren, often deriving much satisfaction in return – all the pleasure and none of the responsibility. The loss of a grandchild can severely damage this sense of purposefulness at a time when they may be feeling redundant in other respects.

As grandparents, we'll not only be grieving the loss of our grandchild – we'll also be grieving just as deeply for our own child's loss. This is one occasion, however, when we're not going to be able to 'make things better' another dent to our self-esteem.

'Survival guilt' is another common experience. We might desperately wish we could have changed places. This challenges how worthwhile our lives are if we can go on living after our grandchild has died.

This all adds up to a recipe for depression. If we're in this situation we should take notice of what's happening to us and, if we're not, we should keep an eye open for forgotten grandparents.

The anticipated death

If we have cared for someone throughout a long final illness we will have been grateful for the time to prepare for the death and to say our goodbyes. We will also, however, know about the anguish of the uncertainty about what might happen. We would have had to find a balance between normal living and behaving as though the end could come at any time. We may have prepared ourselves for the death several times: false alarms.

These situations are often the most painful for all concerned. The carer – anxious and fearful – is often also exhausted; exasperation and resentment may be barely concealed. Patience and concern may become less evident to the dying person who may feel depressed and guilty for causing 'so much trouble'.

Curiously, no matter how much preparation there has been, the actual death always seems to come unexpectedly.

The sudden death

Whether or not the death was expected is one of the key factors in our ability to adjust. With a sudden death we can immediately see how some of the difficulties could have been lessened if – as usually happens – there had been the opportunity for some preparation:

> *Before her death my sister asked to see each of her five brothers and sisters. We talked about how we had been close and trusting with each other, and we also talked about some of our long-standing fights and grudges.*
>
> *I know that the hour she and I spent going over our times together was very important to me. It was one way to say goodbye. And I think it was important and healing for her as well.*

> J. Shapiro, quoted in *Ourselves: Growing Older*, 1989

Much of the grief that follows a sudden death comes from the incomplete relationship that has been left behind. The last chapter of our time together has been torn out and discarded without any opportunity for truths to be revealed, confusions to be explained and doubts to be resolved.

All of us, in our relationships, play a series of roles. Our partner can be a 'counsellor' at breakfast time, a 'stubborn child' at lunchtime and a 'playmate' in the evening. We can respond to them in similar ways to suit our mutual needs.

Some people unfortunately become locked in to a very limited drama which takes over their life – 'abuser-victim', 'nurse-patient', 'young lovers'. When we allow our relationships to become 'hardened' in this way we become severely restricted in how we can express our needs and respond to others.

The 'abuser' becomes incapable of saying 'Sometimes I feel ashamed of the way I treat you' and the 'patient' finds it hard to be strong and supportive. We all know everyone has many hidden aspects to themselves, but we rarely have the privilege of having the full range of their complexity revealed to us.

It is this openness and honesty about our feelings, fears, hopes and needs that mark a strong relationship; we become 'fully known' to each other.

If we have had this complete knowledge of the other person we may feel their loss sharply when they die but we shall, at least, know *who* and *what* we have lost – unlike Lorraine:

> *David was never very demonstrative but in the last couple of years he became very wrapped up in himself: he seemed quite depressed to me. He seemed less interested in the children and began working late quite often – I still wonder if there might not have been another woman. Anyway, the Saturday before it happened we had a big row about going on holiday. I said things I shouldn't and he eventually said – completely out of the blue – that he thought we should separate. He ignored me all day on Sunday.*
>
> *Monday morning he was gone, as usual, when we got up. The police came at three o'clock to say he'd been killed in the train crash – a signal failure. I hadn't even watched the News.*

Lorraine was now left with her children and her grief. However, she was also left with a lifetime of doubts:

◆ Why had David been so unhappy?
◆ What had she failed to do?
◆ Did he really want to leave her?
◆ Had he been seeing someone else?
◆ Had he stopped loving her – and why?
◆ Did he know how much she loved him?
◆ How will the children remember him?

Such a situation as this brings home to us the importance of looking after living relationships so that our 'wholeness' is clear to each other and that we regularly check for changes. When someone close dies there should be as little 'unfinished business' as possible.

The effects of sudden death can be debilitating for the survivor. The bereavement is usually longer and there is more marked physical and emotional signs of distress. There is a condition called 'unexpected loss syndrome' where people are bewildered, socially withdrawn, feeling helpless, distrustful and angry.

> *The bitterest tears shed over graves are for words left unsaid and deeds left undone.*
>
> Harriet Beecher Stowe (1811–96)

Death by violence

The pain and shock of a normal bereavement are intensified if the death was violent – the violence of the act somehow becomes reflected in the sharpness of the grief.

Here are some of the features that frequently mark out this sort of death.

◆ The cause of the death came unexpectedly from outside; other sudden deaths are usually preceded by some ill health or anxiety, but with these deaths – fatal accidents or murder – there was no time to take stock of what was happening – not even the opportunity to recognise that death was imminent. This goes against our deep sense that we ought to have even a short time to put things in order and say goodbye.

◆ There is usually some explanation for the death, which could involve blame – the drunk driver, the fanatical terrorist, the inadequate safety arrangements. This can bring a third person into our grief work – whether they intended the death or not. We can, understandably, become preoccupied with feelings of recrimination and revenge, which will interfere with our bereavement.

◆ Often violent deaths are accompanied by mutilation of the body. The image that we have of the disfigured dead person will colour our future memories and emphasise their dramatic end. It's little comfort to know that the severity of any mutilation rarely reflects any extreme suffering – in fact the more brutal and overwhelming the trauma the more the victim's response to the shock will protect them from any pain at all. We may ponder on whether it's good or bad that they may not have had any consciousness at all of what happened.

◆ Unlike most other deaths the violent death could usually have been prevented; the closer we were and the more we were able to influence the person's life, the more opportunity we will have to scratch at our own possible responsibility. If we dig deep enough in our fantasies we will always find some way in which we could have changed things.

◆ This is unlikely to remain a private event. There may be some sort of investigation perhaps leading to prosecution: there will be lots of questions, rumours and media interest. The course of our grief can be overlain with an administrative timetable that extends for months or years. Forensic enquiries may prevent an immediate disposal of the body – causing greater distress.

Dealing with a sudden, violent death is often difficult to manage on our own and it may be worth considering professional help if we don't have someone we can talk to.

Suicide

I suppose you feel entirely responsible?

Anon (and just as well)

◆ About 5,000 people commit suicide in the United Kingdom every year.
◆ At least 200,000 people attempt suicide every year.
◆ In the 15–19 age group 750 people in every 100,000 attempt suicide – more than twice as many as ten years ago.
◆ Suicide attempts and successful suicides are increasing faster for young people than any other age group. It's the third most frequent cause of death for young people.
◆ Someone who has previously attempted suicide is more than 1,000 times as likely to try again than someone who has not.

When someone takes their own life they are making a statement that their life was too intolerable to continue. If we were part of that life – sufficiently close to cause us to be bereaved – we may feel that we should and could have affected the outcome, but failed. 'Look what you made me do' is hard enough to bear but 'look what you failed to stop me doing' is harder. We all (well, nearly all) like to think of ourselves as sensitive, caring people; a close suicide knocks all that aside.

With ordinary deaths there is usually a general feeling of goodwill, with everyone wanting to behave well. The circumstances around a suicide may be very different. The time leading to the act itself may have been one of bitterness, disturbed behaviour, anger and broken relationships. There may have been ignored threats about self-harm.

We may find it very hard to deny that we *did*, indeed, share some of the responsibility. Most people close to the dead person will be able to think of something they could have done which might – just – have changed the outcome.

Other people don't like it either – attempted suicide was a criminal offence until the 1960s. There still remains an almost universal taboo against it – maybe because many people will have had fleeting thoughts themselves about it but fought them off: 'If I can put up with life's difficulties, why couldn't he?' It feels like a slap in the face to all of us.

However, it seems wrong to condemn it as an aggressive act – a pointless, attention-seeking gesture intended to hurt us. It takes no account of the person's distress, self-absorption and muddled thinking.

Suicide happens because life is either too much for us or there is not enough to be worthwhile.

Thomas Lambton

Although suicide makes a statement about self-worth, there are three distinct types:

Anger suicide

If we endure extreme injustice, abuse, neglect, bullying or other continual negative experience and, for whatever reason, we feel impotent to respond, there will be a build-up of unexpressed frustration, which will eventually turn into a violent inner rage.

Usually we have ways of complaining, seeking support or simply getting out of the way which will defuse the situation, but some people are:

- ◆ without the confidence or self-esteem to stand up for themselves
- ◆ conditioned by others not to express violent feelings
- ◆ unable to escape.

Eventually there is nowhere where their rage can be contained. The pressure explodes and damages or destroys the only thing that they have any control over – themselves. Typically, because of the intense anger that is driving it, this sort of suicide will be a violent one.

We may feel that there was an aggressive intention to hurt the survivors. If this was so, we can take some comfort from the fact that it was a decision made at a time when they were disturbed and irrational in their thinking

Fear suicide

This is the other side of the coin. Anger suicide happens because 'The world thinks I'm worthless'. Fear suicide is a statement that 'I think I'm worthless'. The basic experience of being oppressed, depressed or hard done by may be similar to anger suicide. However, maybe because of their personality or past experience, these unfortunate people become the victims of a turned-in apathy and hopelessness which feeds on itself. At some point the fear of living will become greater than the fear of dying.

There will be no visible violence – they are beyond the thought that they could make an impact.

Although, again, as survivors we may be drawn into thinking that we are being punished or made to feel guilty, we ought to realise that, according to their distorted sense of reality, they may genuinely have thought that we would be better off without having them and all the worry they were inflicting on us.

Rational suicide

It is possible for people to take their lives in a reasoned, planned way – people suffering from terminal or chronic disease who judge they no longer have sufficient quality of life. Part of their planning, however, will have included the intention of looking after the feelings of their survivors and absolving them from responsibility. The people who cause the most distress usually do it unintentionally by ill-judging their potential for recovery and by not realising how much support there could have been for them.

But that's no comfort...

It may be particularly hard for us to come to terms with our guilt and responsibility. There is no easy way out of this because it may, indeed, be true that if things had been different, the suicide might have been avoided. However, we can't go on trying to account for all the 'if onlys' of life. We've all caused unthinking distress to someone in our lives – but then, our occasional kind word and warm smile has also brought unknown, accidental happiness to others.

The best solution is to allow ourselves guilt feelings only if we actually *wished* the suicide to happen. Otherwise, try not to allow such feelings.

Our neighbours and friends will be sympathetic, but they know how guilty they would feel in our position: maybe they think we *are* to blame. They may be reticent about offering us support – they may even be hostile. If there was no obvious reason for the suicide, people might press us for an explanation – trying to get us to make sense where there is none. Suddenly, the awkward reticence usually associated with death seems cruelly absent; the dead person would have been hard put to give a rational explanation for what they have done – how can we, with our guilt and self-accusations, be expected to come up with an answer.

It is unfair for others to encourage speculation and we have no responsibility for giving a public diagnosis of their state of mind; we should be courteous but firm:

> *I know everyone is looking for an explanation; maybe why she did it will become easier to work out in time – but I'm feeling dreadful, as you'll understand, and that's all I can cope with at the moment.*

On top of all this – to add to our distress – there will be a police investigation where it's possible that we may be initially suspected of murder. The details of the incident will be newsworthy so there may be media interest in family relationships just when we want to be left in peace.

There is evidence that bereavement for survivors of people who have taken their own lives is much harder and that recovery takes longer than with a 'normal' death.

> *We'd been away for the weekend. When we got back on Sunday evening there was a message from him on the answering machine: 'It's teatime on Saturday. Can you come round. There's something important I need to talk to you about.'*
>
> *There was something urgent in his voice, which made me ring immediately. No reply. I went round to the flat. A neighbour had found him hanged that morning. That was three years ago now and not a day goes by without me wondering if I could have made a difference.*
>
> Tom Calder

Suicide is not necessarily the rare event that we suppose:

> *Authorities have estimated that reported suicides may*
> *constitute as little as a quarter of actual suicides. This*
> *discrepancy results from the misclassification of thousands of*
> *deaths each year as automobile or shooting accidents, heart*
> *attacks, accidental drug overdoses or unintentionally fatal*
> *combinations of drugs and alcohol.*
>
> Carol Staudacher, *Beyond Grief*, Souvenir Press 1988

This misclassification can result from the family wishing to avoid the guilt and stigma of suicide, clever concealment by the dead person or a well-meaning conspiracy of doctors, police and family to avoid pain and protect any insurance benefits which would be invalidated by a verdict of suicide.

There's something about the way we feel 'provoked' by a suicide, which draws and binds us to the act; our feeling of self-worth may be dented. It's not uncommon for survivors to feel that because of the way they have been implicated, they themselves are fated to die in the same way. There's something so special about it that it seems we will only 'meet up with' the dead person if we take the same path. Also, because of the immediacy of what has happened, suicide is no longer seen as unthinkable and forbidden, something that happens to others; it becomes an option for us as well. Self-harm can run in families.

There may be a sense of deception. We were not, apparently, as important as we thought in the relationship and we have also, apparently, misjudged the intentions of the dead person. We have 'got things wrong' in a spectacular way and our self-image (and the image we had of the other person) may be seriously damaged.

How can we come to terms with suicide?

◆ Suicide is usually outside most people's experience. We may feel free to interpret the reasons for it ourselves and we are usually wrong. It's worth finding out some information about the subject. We'll discover that the reasons for suicide are complex – usually a lifetime's interaction of personal, social and cultural factors. These are major influences, hard to define and change – we should take some comfort that even the most practised researchers disagree about their relative importance. Who are we, amidst all this complexity, to decide that a major cause of the despair was the sarcastic remark we made last Thursday?

◆ There is no evidence that anyone has been prevented from taking their life by someone restricting the availability of the means for self-harm: if there is a strong enough intention it cannot be thwarted.

◆ Because of the public discomfort about the subject it is harder for someone bereaved by suicide to talk easily about their feelings, and yet – more than with other deaths – there may be a greater urgency to talk. Usually with ordinary deaths it is helpful to talk to someone who knew the dead person. In this situation any overlaying difficulty can be avoided by seeking out someone who never knew the dead person – someone who can give all their empathy to us.

◆ Often a letter has been left behind giving explanations, expressing aggression or despair. This may be read repeatedly for clues and nuances and can be the source of bitter frustration because it is a one-way message. We can do something about that: we can reply to it. This means a full statement showing our understanding of the pain and sharing our feelings about our responsibility, regrets and unfinished business. The process of doing this may clarify our thoughts and uncover unexpected feelings.

◆ People whose spouse has died by suicide should be especially careful when they later wish to enter a fresh long-term relationship. It is not uncommon to seek out someone who needs to be 'cared for' – who has problems that we can 'solve'. In this way we can go some way to 'make up for' our imagined 'faults' which lead to the death. A relationship whose main purpose is solving the unresolved problems of the previous one is doomed to failure.

Extra-marital grief

There are some situations where normal grief feelings are not only ignored but positively discouraged. Many men and women develop extra-partnership attachments to other people. The lover will not be a welcome mourner at the funeral and, because there's likely to have been secrecy, they may have no one to talk to about their distress. This can be a very painful considering how much consolation and support we normally get from our close family. On the other hand, if it is the lover who has died, the person in the partnership will be stranded with their clandestine grief in the middle of day-to-day family life.

There may be similar difficulties when an ex-partner dies. The attachment we had for them may still remain alive even though we separated a long time ago – we may have spent some very good years together. There may be some ambivalence about how much distress we are permitted to show in public. We can only hope that our existing partner understands enough to know how these things work. Will the bereaved partner welcome us to the funeral? If we wish it, it may be a good idea to make discreet enquiries – the chances are that *they* will not know whether we would welcome an invitation.

Grief for pets

> *There is sorrow enough in the natural way*
> *From men and women to fill our day;*
> *And when we are certain of sorrow in store,*
> *Why do we always arrange for more?*
> *Brothers and sisters, I bid you beware*
> *Of giving your heart to a dog to tear.*
> Rudyard Kipling (1865–1936), 'The Power of the Dog'

An outsider might well consider the grief expressed for a dead animal to be a rather shameful indulgence. That is to deny the complexity and depth that many people have in their relationships with pets.

We remember that our cat died when we were seven and how we were upset but had got over it the following day. When the elderly family dog died you and your children had been upset but you couldn't help but feel privately relieved that you wouldn't have to clean up after it again.

Many people, however, invest a great deal emotionally in their pets. Many people without children have an almost parental attachment to their animals. Whilst we may have our own opinion about this, when their pet dies we must not minimise their authentic bereavement – in quality it may be as sharp as the death of a child.

Older people on their own often cling to the physical comfort and company of a pet. The consequent loneliness and isolation can sharpen the grief for the loss of such an animal.

> *Not the least hard thing when they go away from us, these quiet friends (dogs), is that they carry away with them so many years of our own lives.*
>
> John Galsworthy (1867–1933), *Memoirs*

Death in other cultures

> *A soldier going to place flowers on the grave of a fallen comrade met a native [sic] carrying a food-offering to his ancestral tomb. Amused by this superstitious absurdity, the soldier asked him when his ancestors would emerge from the tomb to enjoy their meal.*
>
> *'About the same time as your friend comes up to smell your flowers,' he answered.*
>
> Puckle, *Funeral Customs*, 1926

The traditions associated with death in our European-American culture have been shaped by Christian ideas and practices. These tend to be restrained – solemn even. Funerals are quiet, short affairs – a tear might be shed but feelings usually remain private.

We have much to learn from other cultures that mostly give greater obvious significance to a death. Dying often has a deeper meaning for those who remain and rituals are much more established, lengthy and elaborate. The upheaval in family relationships is noted and changed roles are acknowledged. In rural Crete today, for example, there are regular reminders of death for the whole community:

> *You have the funeral, then a service at nine days, 40 days, three months, six months, nine months and a year. Nowadays,*

most people hold them at the monastery rather than their
village church . . . this morning there were 35 such services – or
rather the 35 names were read out and prayed for at the end
of the morning service which started at 6am and finished
around 10.15 . . . then the people depart to vast rooms with
long tables to eat cakes and pastries and drink coffee . . . There
must have been 2,000 people . . .

Linda Nithavrianakis, 1999

The process of dying, preparing and disposing of the body,
mourning and bereavement are linked to very specific practices;
these make the process of dealing with death a very active one
which engages people in particular ways. The process has a
visibility and presence that often seems much healthier than
our hushed tones and respectful silences.

On the other hand our 'respectability' and our inhibitions
about expressing feelings or religious rituals may make us
horrified at some of the extreme emotions and physical
arrangements for the body; we may not understand different
attitudes to bereavement.

This may lead to discrimination of people from other
ethnic traditions who need to use British health services,
mortuaries, coroners, cemeteries and crematoria.

It's intriguing that those cultures which have clearly-agreed,
shared rituals about grief and mourning 'have an almost
complete absence of "prolonged grief" ' (Rosenblatt, Walsh and
Jackson, 1976).

Hindu death

Practices vary according to caste, region of origin and financial
means.

It is important that death should take place at home; death
in a hospital is likely to cause great distress. Family and friends
will stay at the deathbed throughout the final hours, praying
that the gods will intervene to prevent their loss: there is no
sense of 'acceptance' that death is inevitable.

Relatives might fetch money and clothes for the dying
person to touch before distributing them to the poor.

As the person is about to die he is moved out of bed and
on to the floor: the relatives place basil leaves which have been

dipped in holy Ganges water on the lips of the dying person to purify the body, accompanying this with holy songs. There will be loud shrieks at the moment of death. It is important that *only* the family (of the same sex) should wash and prepare the body. The body is cremated (the same day, or the following day if the death was in the evening) on a funeral pyre lit by the eldest son. There is more singing and wailing while people wait to hear the skull cracking, which shows that the spirit is finally released. The ashes are scattered on flowing water – preferably the Ganges.

During the next 10 to 16 days there is open house with simple refreshments provided for relatives and friends. There are prayers, songs and holy readings. A widow will wipe away her wedding mark and women relatives will wear white saris for the next year. There are further rituals at one, three and six months. Although traditionally widows were normally in mourning for a year it is nowadays reduced to three months.

Jewish death

The dying person reviews their life and may leave an ethical will, which contains messages to their family of their hopes and values.

There should be no undue effort to prolong life or hasten death. Those present at the time of death should hold back their immediate grief and remain in the room. The family arranges the body, covered with a sheet, with the feet pointing towards the door.

Jews should not be involved in the washing of the body; this is left to the funeral director who is called by the Rabbi. Mirrors in the house are covered. The physical body is sacred and should not be embalmed or cut – any severed parts should be buried, unwashed. Organ donation is not encouraged. The body should be buried, not cremated, with some earth from the Holy Land in the coffin.

Gentiles should keep away from the funeral, which should take place within 24 hours of death. Family and friends take the responsibility for filling in the grave.

It is only after the funeral that grief can be expressed and support given to the bereaved. For the first three days the family remain in private: during the next four days friends will visit, bringing food and comfort, and speaking only when spoken to. There are candles and prayers, and Gentiles are now welcome to share the family's grief.

The family will not cut their hair or shave during the next month; during the following ten months there will be weekly prayers. After this time the mourning period is over and further grief is discouraged.

Mourning is also discouraged if the person has not been found, committed suicide, been cremated or was a baby younger than 30 days.

Muslim death

Muslims face death with the same austerity and fervour that they show in life. Death is a time for final judgement on the way someone has lived his life.

The dying person will be keen to show the strength of their faith and will wish to raise themselves in their beds to face in the direction of Mecca. Any continued afterlife is dependent on a thorough preparation of the body by the family at the local mosque and a speedy burial (within 24 hours).

There is a ceremony before the funeral when family and friends are permitted to crowd around the body; they will wish to kiss and touch the face for the last time. The burial is the business of men only; they must hold back their emotions while wrapping the body without touching it.

When it is buried the eyes should face Mecca and a board is placed over the head. Prayers are said in the mosque on the third, seventh and fortieth days after the death. It is considered improper for children to be involved in any of these rituals.

It is the hope of all Muslims who live overseas that their body can be returned home, although the costs involved may make this a problem.

Mourning should last for no more than three days when everyone should be encouraged to 'return to normal'; no one should then talk about death and the deceased person.

Buddhist death

A Buddhist death is a sorrowful but gentler affair. Buddhists believe that our mortal life is just one of many – our subsequent progress being determined by our self-created 'karma' (the way we have lived) and the prayers of others: it is more like a departure for the next stage of a journey.

Because the concept of 'individualism' and attachment to possessions and relationships is alien to Buddhism, the Western sense of loss and bereavement is less sharp and there is more emphasis on wishing the person well (through prayer) in their future lives.

It is important that the body is allowed a period of peace in the time following death for the 'spirit' to move on. Family members wash the body.

The local monks will cast a 'death horoscope' which indicates which prayers are appropriate and when the body is best cremated.

The body is carried in procession with family and friends and is accompanied by music. The body can be buried or cremated – the flames of a funeral pyre are seen as purifying.

Six weeks after its 'previous' death the spirit will attach itself to an embryo at conception to begin its next life. Less fortunate souls will find themselves returned as an animal and the most wretched will reappear as sad or angry ghosts with a lesser hope of advancement towards the ultimate Nirvana.

There will be warm support for bereaved relatives from friends and monks. Mourning lasts for 100 days during which time people should dress in subdued colours.

CHAPTER 6

Looking to the Future

I n the early days after the death we may want to throw off and escape the lethargy and helplessness that have taken hold of us – but we may be mistaken. We'll have known shock, depression and despair in the past and we'll try to rid ourselves of them as we did then. Later we *are* going to have to work positively towards building a new life but, at first, it's probably best to surrender to things.

Go with the flow

When we have 'flu we are biologically programmed to become physically helpless to the extent that we can do nothing other than lie in a warm bed. This is intentional; nature needs our bodies to shut down so that it can concentrate on fighting the virus.

The same is true with the depression induced by bereavement. Our difficulty in concentration and making decisions, feelings of lack of confidence, withdrawal, tiredness, lack of energy and inability to 'get going' – these are all psychologically self-protective. Our depressed behaviour is designed to slow us down in order to take stock of our new, changed situation; our 'symptoms' in this sense are positive – they allow us a breathing space and they give a 'do not disturb' signal to other people.

In the short term we should therefore 'respect' our depression and take advantage of the respite without feeling guilty about it.

The trouble is that if we do not eventually face up to the changes in our life, we can be drawn further down as a long-term protection from reality. By then we may have lost many of our resources to do anything about it – even if we wanted to; this might be the point at which we need help from outside.

'Respecting' our grief means:

♦ being content, especially at first, to be carried along by the depression – it's on our side

♦ setting realistic goals for ourselves – 'I may not be up to going to town for the day, but I can go down the road to the newsagent' – doing too much and failing may make things worse

♦ breaking things down to manageable tasks – 'I can't face answering all 37 letters, but I probably could manage two a day'

♦ we shouldn't be hard on ourselves for forgetting things or leaving tasks undone

♦ we should hold on to the expectation that, even without any effort on our part, the depression will almost certainly lift of its own accord.

Ask yourself 'Would I treat my best friend the way I'm treating myself?'

First-aid for stuck minds

Over the next days and weeks the fresh, scarred feelings of loss are likely to cause anxiety, fear and confusion. For a while our perception of the world may become skewed; we can be over-preoccupied with feelings of hopelessness and despair and we may falsely interpret everything that happens in personal terms.

This happens in any crisis. Normally we have a natural chemical and psychological resilience, which bounces us back to our normal self after a short time and the misery melts away.

However, if the blow is hard enough, if the implications are confusing enough or if the guilt is unbearable enough, our resources for recovery may be severely damaged and, instead of our normal mood and thinking being restored, we may drift into a deepening hole of despair.

This is the point at which 'feeling miserable' becomes 'depression'. Up to now we can be cushioned by relationships, support, hugs, advice, encouragement and kindness. If we slip into a vicious descent into despair, however, our emotional engine may no longer respond to a push-start.

It is not that we risk never being 'cured' of our depression – eventually there will be a (slow) internal recovery. It is rare for even untreated depression not to lift over time. However, in the short term we can become psychologically disabled as well as suffering the pain of despair.

We may have become incapable of directly altering our mood or making sense of our thoughts. We would love to be able to 'pull ourselves together' – but there are things that we *can* do which, indirectly, may spark our body chemistry into action or give a direction towards the return to social and psychological competence.

Do something – anything

> *If you always do what you've always done*
> *You'll always get what you've always got.*
> Alan Cohen, *The Dragon Doesn't Live Here Any More*

> *Advice for a melancholic man: 'Let him take a course in*
> *Chemistry, or a course in Rope-dancing, or a course in*
> *anything to which he is inclined.'*
> Samuel Johnson (1709–84)

The first – and easiest – thing to do is to break free of the featureless, black lethargy that has overwhelmed us. We don't need to think too deeply about this; all we need to do is to create some simple structure to our time and activity. We can, for example, make the simple decision that there will be two parts to our day: in the morning we will remain at home and in the afternoon we will always be out of the house for an hour. A simple enough decision – but already we have given a pattern to our life.

Apart from re-establishing a rudimentary routine this ensures that we are involved in some activity every day. At first this can be unremarkable – walk for half an hour in any direction and then turn round and return home – but it will ensure that we involve ourselves with the outside world instead of being wrapped in gloomy introspection. We will be forced to wonder if we should wear a coat, do we need any shopping, what will we say if we meet a neighbour? It's a simple decision to pick ourselves up and physically place ourselves back in the world for a while every day – no more than that at first.

Apart from turning ourselves into someone who can move regularly between two locations, the importance of getting out of the house is even greater: it gets us moving.

Physical exercise can be our most valuable ally.

◆ The achievement of moving from A to B is proof that we are capable of taking control at a time when we may feel ourselves a helpless victim.

◆ Paradoxically, the more we exercise the less tired we will feel. This is because the 'grief-tiredness' we have been feeling was really a sort of paralysing lethargy – a dull stress-induced tension. When we replace this with 'real', 'exhaustion-tiredness' it is curiously refreshing.

◆ The most important effect of exercise, however, is the way that physical activity affects the chemistry of our brains. Even gentle physical exertion produces endorphins, which act like opiates – producing a sense of euphoria. Even though we've 'manufactured' this sense of well being it reminds us that we are still capable of experiencing pleasure and now that the pathway has been opened up it will be easier next time.

We're not talking about vigorous jogging or 30-mile cycle rides – that's the sort of exercise for those aiming for physical fitness. Sustained walking which leaves us slightly out of breath will be sufficient. Start out modestly and increase activity as you wish. Stop if it seems too much for you; it should always be a pleasure – never a chore.

Keep a grief diary

Early on, when we are emerging from the paralysing impact of shock and we feel at a loss to know what to do next we may have a feeling that we have come to full stop. We seem inactive, unable to put two thoughts together and emotionally dead. This is not so – it's just that we have so many ideas and feelings crowding around that it's hard to grasp any pattern. If we keep our thoughts and feelings in our head they swirl around, become confused and slip away – overtaken by others.

We find it hard to keep hold of ideas and to reflect on the implications of our loss.

One simple way of making some sense of it all is to put our daily life and feelings down on paper. In this way we can keep a record of our activity and catch hold of the progress of our feelings.

At the beginning this can just be a continuous, hour by hour, record of how we are spending our time. Gradually, as we get used to it, we can add comments about how we are feeling about events that happen and reflect on our thoughts.

Eventually as we re-read what we have written, we might feel able to use it to analyse changes in our outlook and note improvements or setbacks in the way we respond to things. Finally, we may wish to use it to plan what we are going to do tomorrow.

Make entries as often as you can – they can be in note form and the structure will suggest itself.

- 'This morning I went...'
- 'Why do I feel so terrified most of the time...'
- 'This afternoon I must make the effort to...'
- 'A TV programme I saw last night left me thinking...'
- 'I finally asked X if he could arrange to sell the car, I felt...'
- 'X told me I was looking much better yesterday...'
- 'I spent all yesterday sorting through her clothes and forgot to keep the diary; is that good or bad?'
- 'I caught myself actually laughing at a joke this afternoon...'
- 'I used the lawn-mower for the first time this afternoon; I didn't realise it was so easy...'
- 'I suddenly began weeping at the chemist's – what was that about? Maybe...'
- 'Her boss came round to see me this morning, I had never realised before that...'
- 'I couldn't have done that last week.'

A diary is useful because it makes us notice things, which may otherwise be unremarkable; putting thoughts and feelings into precisely what is happening. Although when we're making entries, they are 'snapshots', when we go back and read them we are likely to see a changing – hopefully positive – pattern. Finally, the diary can be kept as a graphic memoir of an important time of our life.

The *activity* involved may appeal to bereaved men in particular. We are much more comfortable about organisation and structure: Dr Johnson suggested to his publisher, James Elphinstone, after the death of Elphinstone's mother:

> *There is one expedient by which you may, in some degree, continue her presence. If you write down minutely what you remember of her from your earliest years, you will read it with great pleasure, and receive from it many hints of soothing recollection when time shall remove her yet further from you, and your grief shall be matured to veneration.*

Don't listen to strange thoughts...

In the early depths of bereavement when we are reeling from the loss there is only one thing that we can depend upon – our thinking may be distorted. In normal times, we are able to depend upon our thought processes and intuition to give us an accurate account of reality. We get used to 'trusting our instinct' – we are usually right. Now we are tricked into trusting thoughts and feelings which have been skewed by our grief.

In this way we can easily be led to believe blatant lies about ourselves.

◆ 'My life is effectively over now.'
◆ 'I caused her to die. I don't deserve to be happy again.'
◆ 'I shall never be able to do that: it's beyond me.'
◆ 'I'm useless.'
◆ 'It would be a betrayal to even think about looking for a new relationship.'

These mischievous, trouble-making notions are artificially created by our vulnerable, hurt minds. They are all the more dangerous because they have a deceptive plausibility about them – we can't actually deny that they *could* be true. They also creep up on us unawares and declare themselves shamelessly and without any argument. We may be too hurt to resist.

If we do come upon one of these 'devilish agitators' it's important to give it a hard time – challenge it.

- 'How do you know?'
- 'What's your evidence?'
- 'I refuse to listen.'
- 'Would I have thought this a year ago?'
- 'Is there a simpler explanation?'
- 'Clear off when I'm feeling like this!'

Some people's thoughts can be even more deceptive:

- 'No, I'm feeling fine!'
- 'I just want to get the house sold and move away: I'll be alright then.'
- 'I've got to be strong for the sake of the children.'

These are false-positive ideas, which are equally untrustworthy.

It's best at a time of crisis to distrust *any* unusual or strongly held thoughts or feelings for the time being – especially any extreme negative idea. It's just possible that the message is, indeed, true – but we are in no fit state to judge at the moment. We'll be better served at present by indecision and quiet reflection. It might be worth including thoughts about any similar questions in your diary.

Thoughts to distrust

When we are under stress one of the first casualties is subtlety. Our normal ability to distinguish shades of feelings is in shock and the fine-tuning in our responses gets stuck. At these times we are in danger of distorting the way we feel. The following are signals we should look out for in our thoughts and attitudes; they are almost always untrue, very unhelpful and they will interfere with our bereavement. We won't be able to stop them coming into our heads but we should not make them welcome and we should refuse to entertain their presence.

- Any statement that doesn't rely on evidence: 'I can't explain it – I just feel it's the right thing to do.'
- Me, the victim: 'Everything I touch seems to turn out bad.'
- Any gross self-criticism: 'Marrying me ruined his life.'
- Any sentence with the words 'ought', 'should', 'must',

'always', 'never', 'nobody': 'I ought to be back at work.'

◆ Extreme pessimism: 'I don't think I'll ever be able to manage properly!'

◆ Any exaggeration: 'We never had a cross word in 25 years.'

◆ Assuming the whole responsibility: 'If I'd put my foot down about her moving to London, she would have been 100 miles away when the bomb went off.'

◆ Fantasising: 'If only I had enough money to buy them a bigger house, I could move in with them and look after the children while she's at work – if only I could win the lottery.'

◆ Always expecting the worst: 'No, I'll just quietly curl up and wait to die.'

◆ Any underestimation: 'I've never been able to cook and I never will!'

◆ Drawing factual conclusions from vague feelings: 'The place seems empty without him: I'll feel better when it's sold!'

◆ Any description that is all 'good' or all 'bad': 'Everything about the funeral was a complete disaster!'

◆ Making generalisations: 'Everybody avoids me: nobody is interested in me now that she is dead.'

◆ Any discounting of our achievements: 'So what – I used to hoover *every* day.'

◆ Labelling people: 'We haven't told him, he wouldn't understand – he's got learning difficulties, you know.'

◆ Any negative self-labelling: 'What do you expect, I'm useless at everything.'

Make *some* changes

We know now that we should resist making big changes in our lives at this time. However, there is positive value in making some small, but symbolic, alterations to our surroundings and the way we live.

We can understand the vehement concern a bereaved parent has with 'keeping his room exactly as it was'. Generally, however, there can be something very unhealthy about an obsession to preserve things the way the dead person left them. Even a mild inclination to do this is dangerous because it becomes more and more difficult to go back on the idea. We can find ourselves stuck in a world where 'nothing has happened' – and where the flow of our grief has become arrested.

It can be helpful, when the time seems right, deliberately to make some changes which are *not* fundamental but which are a token acknowledgement that our lives are changed:

- re-arrange or replace some of the furniture
- have a spring-clean and clear out unwanted rubbish
- buy some new clothes
- alter your daily routine in some small way.

The idea is not to put the past behind us – but to stop it forming itself into a mental shrine.

There's a time and place for everything.

> One day when I was coming home from shopping in town, I rested on a bench in the park where we used to sit before her illness. I began to think about our times together. This happened again later in the week and before I knew it that park bench became a quiet, safe haven where I could think about mother, the past and the future.
>
> Annabel Irving

We'll not be able to compartmentalise our thoughts at first; our loss may be ever present. However, as time goes by there is much to be said for having a special time and place where we can give special, uninterrupted attention to our thoughts. It may be a good idea for this 'safe haven' to be out of the home – away from day-to-day distraction.

This is not to put our feelings at arm's length but, rather, to give ourselves the opportunity to focus on our thoughts more intensely. If we can do this away from home it allows us to continue living with less grief distraction.

How can we tell things are improving?

Our progress through grief can be so slow that change can be indistinct. One way of pinning down our emotional progress is to look occasionally at the following statements. It's unlikely we

could have owned any of them during the first time of shock.
When we can respond positively to most of them we can be
sure that we're moving forward.

◆ I'll always remember the time when...
◆ I have decided I am going to do the following...
◆ I spend much less time caught up with negative or self-
destructive thoughts...
◆ I would never have guessed that I would be able to...
◆ It's been awful, but the one important thing I have learned
is...
◆ I can talk about her in the past tense without a feeling of
despair...
◆ I've changed: I've become...
◆ I can enjoy pleasant memories of our time together...
◆ I was useless when it happened but at least now I can...
◆ I can smile and laugh without feeling bad about it...
◆ I'm beginning to be interested in other things and other
people...
◆ I'm looking forward to...
◆ Although my memories will last forever, I feel I can finally
say goodbye.

Our preoccupation with our distress will begin to fade.
Sometimes something funny will happen to us, just as it used
to. Sometimes we'll recall something hilarious that happened in
the past. When that happens, we should go ahead and laugh if
it feels funny. We won't be desecrating our loved one's
memory – we'll be re-creating something of the life we used to
have.

Food and sleep

> *All griefs with bread are less.*
> George Herbert (1593–1633) *Outlandish Proverbs*

We'll have plenty of helpful enquiries about whether we're
eating properly or whether we're getting enough sleep. Such
concern may seem unnecessary – even faintly condescending.

However, the truth is that when we are overwhelmed with
loss our body stops giving a high priority to its own

maintenance; all our energy becomes focused on our immediate grief. This is fine in the short term but over the days and weeks that follow, poor nutrition and lack of sleep will actually increase our vulnerability to the effects of our loss.

We cannot rely on our appetite to keep us well fed, so we must do so consciously – or be reminded.

Sleeping patterns can be disrupted in the same way. It may be that for a very short time – days rather than weeks we can benefit from some prescribed sleeping tablets.

Relaxation

The tension and stress of bereavement are likely to be reflected in aches and tension in our muscles, which will make us irritable and even more depressed. Just as exercise dissipates the stress, so relaxation can achieve a similar effect.

There are many ways of achieving physical calm – yoga, meditation, aromatherapy, visualisation. It's important to choose the method with which we feel most comfortable. There are classes and study groups as well as self-help videos and audio-tapes.

However, there are some simple exercises which we can do ourselves every day, which will not only give us a short cut to relaxation, but will help us keep active, providing that we're not physically unfit.

Exercise

The only cure for grief is action.
G. H. Lewes, *Life of Lope De Vega*

What possible connection can there be between exercise and dealing with grief?

There are three possible links:

◆ Emotional stress and physical tension are closely related. By imposing muscular tension through exercise the physical relaxation that follows has the effect of reducing our *mental* tension or depression.

◆ One of the effects of depression is that the world becomes oppressive and our power to affect things seems to have been removed. By setting (even a limited) physical goal – a walking destination, for example – we gain a sense of achievement which can help to restore our feeling that we are capable.

◆ Exercise also releases chemicals in the brain which can ease pain and distress. This can give us back a feeling of mental well-being – at least for a while.

Exhaust yourself

Most houses have their own gym: it's called a staircase.

This exercise involves running upstairs (mine has 15 treads) ten times, as hard and energetically as you can – it doesn't matter if that's not very much. Your movement in coming down should be the opposite – as if you were a marionette on strings flopping as lightly as possible from step to step.

Stretch yourself

Lie on a bed with your feet and hands supported.

Slowly raise your extended right leg – keeping your right big toe as close to the wall opposite as possible, point into the corner of the wall and ceiling and try to scrape the ceiling with your toe until you reach a point directly above your head. (You'll know when you have reached it because you'll be too uncomfortable to continue.) Instead of lowering your leg let gravity make it flop heavily on to the bed.

Repeat with your left leg and repeat both five times.

Do the same with your right and left arms, pointing, stretching, raising and dropping ten times.

Deep muscle relaxation

A basic technique which is easy to learn and remember and can be practised at almost any time when you are not going to be disturbed.

It's best to lie flat on the floor or a bed with your arms at your side. The idea is to tighten muscles for a count of three and then, slowly, allow yourself to feel the tension draining away as you relax them. Move in a sequence from the hands to the shoulder and then from the toes to the head.

- Make tight fists: relax.
- Tighten the arm muscles (excluding the hands): relax.
- Try to make your shoulders touch your ears: relax.
- Screw up your toes: relax.
- Point your feet away from you so that they are parallel with your legs: relax.
- Stretch your leg muscles by pointing your toes towards your head: relax.
- Tighten your thigh muscles by pressing the back of your knees towards the floor: relax.
- Clench your buttocks together: relax.
- Tightly hold in your stomach muscles: relax.
- Press the small of your back against the floor: relax.
- Tighten your chest muscles by taking in, and holding, a deep breath: relax.
- Try to make your shoulders touch your ears (again): relax.
- Stretch your chin towards the ceiling: relax.
- Bury your chin in your chest: relax.
- Clench your teeth and press your lips tightly together: relax.
- Close your eyes as hard as you can: relax.
- Raise your eyebrows as far back as you can: relax.
- Screw up all your face muscles: relax.

You should now be feeling relaxed. If you are aware of any leftover tension repeat the relevant part of the exercise.

The whole exercise should take about 20 minutes. If you want to 'feel the benefit' do it during the day: if you do it in bed at night, you will almost certainly be asleep in 15 minutes.

Timed breathing

Now that your muscles are relaxed you can do something about reducing further tensions.

Still lying on your back with your arms at your sides, take in a slow breath through your nose, silently counting five seconds – 'one-thousand-and-one, one-thousand-and-two...'

Now hold your breath for a count of five, slowly breathe out through your mouth for a count of five and count five before breathing in again. Repeat this sequence ten times.

Self-hypnosis

> *Every day in every way I am getting better and better.*
>
> Émile Coué

Following on from one or all of the exercises above we can make use of our ability to relax to help us get rid of further stresses and negative thoughts.

When we relax completely we are very near to the trance-like state evoked by hypnosis. This is near the point where our consciousness meets our sub-consciousness – that 'floating' state we are in when we wake up from sleep. This is a useful area because the traffic of thoughts between the two states is particularly easy; 'deliberate', imagined thoughts can be transformed into settled, 'natural' attitudes. Normally, a hypnotherapist will be more powerful in making suggestions about such new attitudes, feelings and behaviours but, in a milder form, we can do it ourselves.

The idea is to try to get rid of negative ways of thinking, to protect ourselves from hurt and to strengthen our self-confidence. Before you start, choose something about yourself which you would like to change: something about your attitudes, your level of functioning, your preoccupations or your anxieties. We'll use the example of being able to face groups of people without fear.

- ◆ Find a comfortable position – sitting or lying down. When you have achieved a relaxed and semi-drowsy state, slowly visualise a calm setting. It should be remote from your familiar surroundings, where you can feel comfortable and completely at ease – preferably a real place you have visited: a beach, a landscape, a room or some other imagined scene. You should be standing outside and slightly above the scene with some shallow steps leading down to it.
- ◆ Spend some minutes looking around, enjoying the scene, sounds, smells and memories.
- ◆ Slowly descend the steps, pausing a few seconds on each one – there will be half a dozen. At each step think the words 'deeper', 'deeper still', 'still deeper...'
- ◆ At the bottom, finally 'in' the scene, you should be in a mild, pleasant, relaxed 'trance'.

◆ As you look about you, say to yourself confidently (according to your example) 'I feel comfortable in the company of other people'.

◆ Drink in the pleasure of your imagined scene as you repeat the suggestion several times, with pauses in between. Look around at the imagined strangers about you, smiling warmly at them.

◆ When you feel completely at ease with your self-suggestion in this safe setting, hold on to your confidence and imagine yourself in another situation where you would normally have a problem – for example, a social evening where you know people are going to be uncomfortable about mentioning your partner's death. Imagine the assured person you were before – now completely at ease with people's embarrassment. What would this new 'assured' person say to them?

◆ Now go back to your safe, happy setting and repeat your suggestion a few more times.

◆ Turn round and slowly climb up the steps – this time telling yourself 'lighter', 'lighter still', 'even lighter'.

◆ Open your eyes and slowly come back to the 'real' world.

This is an exercise you can use in many different ways. Decide on the positive suggestion you want to make to yourself, repeat it with confidence in a safe, imagined place, keep the assured feeling and imagine a more challenging environment. Slowly return by way of the reassuring safe setting.

Don't be afraid that you'll get stuck or that being interrupted is 'dangerous' – you'll be in charge all the time.

Make sure that your suggestion is wholly positive. For example it's no good telling yourself, 'I mustn't worry about meeting new people'.

What you wish to work on is up to you:

◆ loneliness
◆ anxiety
◆ fear of going out
◆ being assertive
◆ self-esteem.

You should be fairly calm to start with. It just won't work if you're in a bad mood or feeling destructive (you'd do better to try some vigorous exercise or talk out your feelings with a friend). Self-hypnosis will only work if you are hoping it will.

Written positive affirmations

> *We are not moved by events, but by the views we take of them.*
>
> Epictetus (*c.* 55–135 AD)

Consider the important parts of your life – particularly those areas which preoccupy your thinking. Compose some statements which reframe your thoughts in a positive way. Two rules:

◆ make them short, straightforward and clear
◆ make them believable and attainable.

Write them down and add a sentence which amplifies and justifies what you have written – making them as personal to you as possible. Read them aloud to yourself regularly and add to the list. Here are some examples.

◆ I deserve all that is good in life...
◆ I forgive myself for...
◆ I am free to...
◆ I accept myself the way I am.
◆ I wish to let go of all bad feeling about the past.
◆ In the future, I look forward to...
◆ I love myself and deserve to be loved.
◆ I have the strength and energy to overcome difficulties.
◆ I will allow myself a daily treat.
◆ I will take care of my health.
◆ I will be kind and generous to myself.
◆ I will seek and enjoy warm, loving relationships.

We should aim to develop 'the undisturbed calmness of mind' described by ancient philosophy. We can do this by encouraging:

> *Friendliness towards the happy*
> *Compassion for the unhappy*
> *Delight in the virtuous*

Indifference towards the wicked.

Patanjali, Indian sage and author

The Deborah Kerr theory

Whenever I feel afraid, I whistle a happy tune...
(Rodgers and Hammerstein, *The King and I*, 1956)

...there is nothing either good or bad, but thinking makes it so...

Shakespeare, *Hamlet*

The problem with the feelings that make up our grief is that they will not be rushed. We haven't got the resources to 'pull ourselves together' or 'snap out of it'. When other people make such suggestions – and they usually do it non-verbally – there's something peculiarly insulting about it.

However, we can escape temporarily from the oppressive dreariness of our thoughts for short periods reasonably easily.

We all know that our moods affect the way we appear to others. When we are feeling miserable our posture closes up, our head and shoulders drop and we avert our gaze; it is as though we were rolling up into a ball – like a hedgehog – to protect ourselves from the world.

What is not so well known is that the reverse is also true. Not only does our mood affect our appearance, but the way we hold ourselves and how we present ourselves to the world can have a significant effect on the way we feel.

Choose a time when you are feeling reasonably at ease and try the following experiment. Sit in a comfortable, easy chair and draw your knees up towards your chest; clasp your legs with your arms and lower your forehead against your knees. Sit like this for half a minute and then say – meaning it: 'I feel really happy.' It's nearly impossible to get the words out and even more difficult for your face to look pleased.

Now try the opposite. Sit up straight, head upright, arms at your side and legs slightly apart, feet on the floor. After a while try saying – with feeling – 'I feel really miserable today'. Again there's something about our open, confident physical posture which resists any association with depressive thoughts.

This could be because there is some reverse chemical action between our physical attitude and our brain. More likely, the effect is caused by a long-developed learned association between our feelings and appearance – just as we can't help looking sad or happy when we feel that way, so we are drawn to *feel* the way that we look.

The implications of this are not profound. There is no question of 'recovering' from depression with some programme of posturing and pulling faces. However, for short periods, in the depths of our grief, we can induce short spells of well-being, which can remind us of our temporarily lost ability to feel good. Here's how.

The task is to walk for an hour. Find a route – preferably one that is new to you – where you are unlikely to meet anyone you know. There should be no destination to distract you.

The idea is that you should walk for half an hour, turn round and then walk back.

What is important is *how* you walk. Your head should be erect and your spine straight – as though you were being suspended by a marionette's string from the back of the top of your head. You're three centimetres taller than usual; it's as though your feet are just touching the floor.

Hold your shoulders back and swing your arms in rhythm with your stride, which should be long enough to cause some slight strain on your calf muscles. Your pace should be brisk – sufficient to cause a glow of perspiration – without you becoming out of breath.

People you meet will note how confident and assured you appear. Can you manage a slight smile? Don't stop – but make an effort to be curious about what's happening en route.

When you get back, have a cup of tea and notice how you've have been feeling.

It will soon pass, as your real world returns, but you may be reassured that you still have the potential for positive living. Repeat three times a week, after meals. Remember:

When I fool the people I fear.
I fool myself as well...

Becoming more confident

> *In a study on self-esteem using a scale of 100, it was found that an average person's self-esteem was in the 70s and generally a bereaved person's was in the teens.*
>
> Thomas Lambton

Lack of confidence affects:

our thinking:

- ◆ I just can't make up my mind
- ◆ It's too difficult
- ◆ I'd never be able to cope

our feelings:

- ◆ I'll never match up to the rest of them
- ◆ I feel so stupid and frustrated at my shyness
- ◆ I'm sick of the way they always manage to come out on top

our behaviour:

- ◆ merging into the background
- ◆ dependency on other people
- ◆ avoiding changes in our lives

our physical appearance:

- ◆ hunched-up stance
- ◆ no direct eye contact
- ◆ anxious, wary look.

Confidence has many aspects. We have many parts to our lives and we may be lacking confidence in some and very much more at ease in others; surprisingly, we also might find ourselves more self-assured in 'difficult' areas – relationships for example – than in apparently less demanding situations like walking into a doctor's waiting room.

Most people aim to give an impression of self-confidence and mostly succeed. Nobody is assured in all areas of their lives.

If we give out signals that we lack confidence, people will treat us accordingly and this will only add to our feelings of inadequacy.

Learn about assertiveness. If you can't attend a course, there are many helpful books (*A Woman in Her Own Right* by Ann Dickson is highly recommended for both women and men).

It's no good simply trying to 'read' or 'think' ourselves more confident. We will only become more self-assured by practice, facing our apprehensions, making mistakes and learning to shrug off setbacks. We are usually most conscious about our diffidence when we are confronted with testing situations. Take advantage of everyday encounters to try out your emerging assurance.

> *No matter. Try again. Fail again. Fail better.*
> Samuel Beckett (1906–89)

- Deliberately initiate casual conversations with shop assistants.
- How 'powerful' can you appear to bank cashiers?
- Talk about the weather to someone in the bus queue.
- For a change *you* ask the hairdresser where *they* are going for their holidays.
- Organise things so that you are regularly in contact with other people.
- Become a volunteer in a charity shop or meals on wheels.
- Get to know the neighbours.
- Write a three-page letter to a friend or relative every week.
- Search out opportunities to be kind to someone.

Even being amongst a crowd of people is better than nothing. Being alone for lengthy periods will tend to shrivel up our social skills – we'll become wrapped up in your own concerns.

There are two sorts of self-confident people:

- miserable people who don't care about other people because they've never learned to like themselves
- nice, friendly people whose assurance is rooted in respect for others because they respect themselves.

We, of course, are in the second group. (It would be a commendable act of kindness for you to find someone from the first group and take them under your wing.)

This element of *respect* is crucial. We will only understand this if we value ourselves and are therefore happy to be 'known' to the world. If we think ourselves worthless and undeserving of attention we will avoid confrontations and retreat from relationships. An important part of increasing self-confidence, therefore, is to find out what is likeable about us and to feed it regularly by:

◆ looking after ourselves physically
◆ taking care with our appearance
◆ finding ways of treating ourselves regularly – especially if we can include a friend
◆ seeking out new, undiscovered pleasures.

If we think badly about ourselves, we should try to work out who gave us that idea; confidence is natural (have you ever seen a cat without self-esteem) and if we lack it, it is because someone has removed it. This usually happens in our vulnerable childhood or youth. We know who it was. It wasn't our responsibility.

We can try to rebuild our disabled self-esteem by trying to understand what *caused* that person to damage us. Try to be generous and forgiving towards them and then to put it all behind us. We all have the resources within us to give up being victims and all the tedious baggage involved. We have the right to reinvest all this negative energy in new possibilities.

What sort of a person would we really like to be? (Yes, we can.)

How to do things

Early on in bereavement we can be overwhelmed by a tangle of problems requiring decisions. We can easily fall into an empty daily routine which is comforting in its predictability but which encourages us to put off doing tasks that need attention. Indeed part of depression is a protective defence against doing *anything* in a world which has become overwhelming.

Because our minds are so busy it's hard to retain the full agenda of tasks waiting to be completed. What we lack in cogent thought, however, we usually, now, make up for with *time*. Time to make a list.

Rather than just muddle on, it can be quite useful to organise the process. Talk to someone who knows you – someone you respect. Ask them if they would sit down with you to help you clarify your thoughts about what needs to be done. It might be a good idea to meet on neutral territory where you will be undisturbed.

Have a large sheet of paper and, between you, think about all the areas of your life that may need attention. Write everything down, however silly it may seem, without comment or discussion. Don't be discriminating or sensible; at this stage 'Replace the dish cloth' can sit easily beside 'Should I remarry?' Try not to think too much about what you are writing. See how long you can make it.

Spend a few minutes silently going through what you've written down. Now, look fairly briskly at each item and sort them into four categories.

◆ A: Important action urgently required.
◆ B: Urgent but low importance.
◆ C: High importance but not urgent.
◆ D: No importance and not urgent.

Go through the 'urgent' list and score each item on a scale of one to ten according to their priority, not their importance. Replying to your granddaughter's letter of sympathy may be much more urgent than selling the house. Once you have the 'urgent' things out of the way you will remove a lot of the fear and anxiety and you'll find it easier to concentrate on the rest which is likely to be more important.

Now that you have some order in your affairs you might feel relaxed enough to decide straight away what action needs doing. Decide exactly what you're going to tackle first and when you're going to deal with it. Put it in your diary, and set it aside, moving on to the next item.

◆ Some parts of your list will be harder to deal with. You may need to break things down into columns of pros and cons. Just writing down the lists may well clarify your unconscious wishes – and it's often wise to trust these hunches.
◆ Imagine what each course of action would involve. Try and visualise your life in three months or five years time. How will it have been affected by moving house, getting remarried, going to live in Spain, keeping or spending your savings?
◆ It's hard for us to keep in mind how things can change with unexpected impacts. Babies are born, friends move away, there are unexpected crises and health can change for

the worse.

When you've done all the weighing up, talking around and imagining alternative outcomes and you're satisfied that you haven't missed out some important factor, make your decision – as dispassionately as possible but don't neglect your intuition.

Having decided to tackle a particular problem area ask some specific questions.

◆ Is it really my responsibility to be thinking about this?
◆ Is it essential for me to think about this now?
◆ How will I know when I have completed it?
◆ How do I expect to feel afterwards?
◆ What worries do I have about achieving it?
◆ How can I reduce my anxiety about it?
◆ Can I imagine myself actually doing it?
◆ What might I say?
◆ What problems might there be?
◆ Where do I start and what further steps need I take?

Then do it.

Five rules for getting things done

◆ Don't try to solve the insoluble. For example, if the post-mortem was inconclusive there may probably be a good argument to let it pass rather than fruitlessly chase after 'the truth' for the rest of your life.

◆ Tackle one problem at a time, but have the security of knowing that the others are not urgent and they won't be forgotten. You can then switch off your thoughts about them and concentrate on the work in hand (20 per cent of problems take up 80 per cent of our energy).

◆ You *will* complete this task successfully. Under no circumstances will you give up if things start to go badly. It is imperative that you can show an achievement. If, before you start, you think that there is a risk that you might not manage it, go back to your list and replace it with one that you can manage.

◆ If we have a choice it is usually more effective – and easier – to concentrate on changing ourselves rather than other people.

◆ We don't always have to come up with some action plan: *doing nothing* is an option. After thinking about it, we might decide that the benefits aren't worth the energy required to achieve them. In the same way we might choose to put up with a situation if it is only going to be temporary. Doing nothing is only dangerous if it comes about through indecision.

Congratulate yourself and, after a rest, go back to your list. If you feel able, try to put the rest of the items into some sort of priority order and make a start on the next task.

As further jobs to be done occur to you, add them to the master list at the appropriate level of urgency.

Let the list take charge of you for the time being. As your competence to make decisions is restored, you can then take back control.

A relationship review

> Say not in grief that he is no more,
> But in thankfulness that he was.

Jewish prayer

After the first shock of bereavement we often have a muddle of memories, feelings and fears. A useful way of taking stock of the past, present and future is to try to review our lost relationship and ask some questions about our present and future situation. It sounds obvious – but without setting aside some time and focusing on details, we sometimes find it hard to get to grips with our feelings and anxieties. Reality becomes much sharper when we set about converting vague feelings into words. We don't know how we feel until we find the words to describe it.

Try going through the following questions and answering each one with a couple of sentences. Even better, write your answers down. A biography of your life together will emerge. Other thoughts will occur to you, which you can also include.

The act of putting together this relationship story will give you a reference point to return to. You will be able to notice changes in your feelings and ideas. It will also be a useful way of recording your 'history' – as the years go by, memories fade; this will remain to refer to. Such an exercise also helps you give a 'completeness' to your relationship, which will eventually help with the task of 'moving on'.

- ◆ I remember when I first met...
- ◆ My first impressions of...
- ◆ What do I know about...'s life before we met?
- ◆ What was my life before we met?
- ◆ What did my family think of...?
- ◆ What did ...'s family think about me?
- ◆ What was it like – the beginning of our relationship?
- ◆ What difficulties did we have?
- ◆ The story of our time together...
- ◆ The things I shall most miss about... now that s/he's gone are...
- ◆ What was ...'s proudest achievement
- ◆ What did... fall short of achieving?
- ◆ When did the events leading to the final illness first begin?
- ◆ How did the illness affect...?
- ◆ How did... regard death?
- ◆ Was... able to say all that s/he wanted to me?
- ◆ What fears do I have for the future?
- ◆ What strengths do I have to face future difficulties?
- ◆ If I need help from others, where can I find it?
- ◆ Do I think, in time, I will want another relationship like the one I had with...?
- ◆ How could a future relationship be different?
- ◆ In what ten practical ways will my life now be different?
- ◆ What difficulties will there be about making these changes?
- ◆ What are my feelings about each of these?
- ◆ What would... be encouraging me to do now if s/he were alive?

These are only suggested cues: you'll know what the other questions are.

Discover who we are now

Strangely, learning to be alone is an important step in learning

> *to heal our loneliness.*
> Susan Jeffers, *Thoughts of Power and Love*, 1997

Having given some attention to ourselves in the context of the previous relationship, it might be worth focusing on us as individuals *now*. The greater our loss, the more our sense of our 'self' is likely to be dented. Our first feelings in relation to the outside world will be those of lack of confidence and incompetence. We need to rebuild a new 'self' which will:

◆ be comfortable and at ease with our feelings
◆ be satisfied with our own 'worth'
◆ be able to mix easily with other people
◆ take a pride in our skills and aptitudes
◆ have a sense of physical well-being.

To achieve this we need to be able to work through our hurt and pain to build a new life for ourselves in which our lost partner has no part. We need to recover those parts of ourselves from the dead person which we gave up to them or never developed in the comfort of our dependence.

◆ We need to see ourselves as a social individual who wants new and improved relationships with others on our own terms.
◆ We need to be able to make an honest assessment of our potential in work or leisure activities.
◆ We need to be aware of our health and fitness.

When we feel that it's time to begin to let go of the past it's worth taking stock of our assets and potential. Ask yourself the following questions; take your time and write down your answers. Better still find someone to go through the questions with you who will ask you to expand.

◆ Write down five key strengths in your personality, which have served you well throughout your life (e.g. honesty, punctuality, dependability). Describe an occasion when each of these has been evident.
◆ How have you changed during your last relationship?
◆ Describe your social abilities before you met the person you have just lost (e.g. suspicious, easy to get on with, shy).
◆ Do you feel confident about meeting other people?

- How far were you dependent in your social life on the person who has died?
- What attracted people to you in the past?
- What qualities did you look for in other people?
- Has there been a common strand running through previous relationships?
- How would other people have described you before you met the person who has died?
- Write down your skills (practical, intellectual, artistic). Which please you most?
- What are your 'blind spots'? If they are important, what can you do about them?
- What do you think about your appearance? Is it important to you? Do you think it's important to other people? If so, what do you need to do?
- In what practical and emotional ways will you miss the dead person? How will you manage?
- Do you need:
  - the approval of other people?
  - to be successful?
  - to be dependent?
  - to be perfect?
  - to get what you want?
  - to have power?

When you have worked through these questions, write down anything that has surprised you or which you think will be important to keep in mind for your new future life.

Grieving doesn't mean we can't feel pleasure

Grief is about adjustment to those parts of our lives and feelings which have been affected by the loss of someone close. There are, however, other aspects of our lives which will remain unaffected. There will, at first, be a gloomy despair which will seep into everything that happens to us, but once we have adjusted to the first shock, we ought soon to be able to recover our ability to enjoy some positive pleasures that are not associated with the loss.

Associations are complex things – only *we* will know the areas that are 'safe' for us, but if we remember the things we used to enjoy we should be able to find some activity to turn to for some respite from our negative thoughts.

The trouble is that we find it hard to experience pleasure without feeling some sense of betrayal – what will other people say if they catch us laughing? However, we know how we feel; it's perfectly possible to be desolate at the loss of a partner *and* to enjoy a meal or a walk in the country. It's important that we hang on to things that can still make us feel good. It's easy to get 'addicted' by habit to gloom; finding small pleasures are the first steps to regaining a new wholeness.

We should also go out of our way to notice our achievements and give ourselves credit for even small improvements in our functioning. Noticing progress in the past helps us see hope for the future. If we find ourselves taking some pleasure in our brooding weakness, it may be difficult, but it is imperative that we give ourselves a slapped wrist. We have enough on our plate trying to emerge from grief – we must resist being seduced by it.

And now for something completely different...

> People are always blaming their circumstances for what they are. I don't believe in circumstances. The people who get on in the world are the people who get up and look for the circumstances they want, and, if they can't find them, make them.
>
> George Bernard Shaw (1856–1950),
> *Mrs Warren's Profession*

The closer our relationship has been, the more likely it will be that all parts of our lives will have some resonance with our loss. One way of breaking free of these constant reminders is to become involved in something that is *new* to us as an individual and had no part in the previous relationship. There will be no associations or memories connected with it and it will be 'a place to go' to try out our new 'aloneness'.

It's preferable if it is straightforward, undemanding, and non-competitive. We should be able to do it without support, without much fuss, and it should have some value or end product. We've all got things in the back of our minds that we'd rather like to do 'one day':

- take up cycling
- learn how to knit
- take up embroidery
- go to an auction
- write a novel
- help with adult literacy
- start going to the gym
- get a job
- become a volunteer – Citizens Advice Centre, Samaritans, Relate
- learn a new language
- learn meditation
- work for a charity
- go somewhere completely new
- buy a motorbike
- be a voluntary car driver
- help in a day centre or hospital
- learn car maintenance
- help at the local school.

It's important that we don't feel disrespectful or guilty about taking pleasure in life. At first we will have no stomach for it but there is no reason why someone suffering deep loss should not take pride in an achievement or begin to enjoy themselves.

If we set aside an hour or two every day for such activities we will not only find some respite from our grieving but they can become a way of levering ourselves back to independent living.

Know who your friends are

> *The only way to have a friend is to be one.*
>
> Ralph Waldo Emerson (1803–82)

'If there's anything I can do...anything!' is not an offer we can rely on. Everyone means it when they say it but the use-by date on the offer may well have expired the following day.

Most people *will* mean it and you will know who they are. Ideally they should be people who are relatively unaffected by the death – probably not relatives – but who have had some experience of being bereaved. They may or may not necessarily be 'friends' (although they may become so).

We need to be able to trust them with confidences – many of the things we will want to talk about are intensely personal.

We need to respect their opinions and advice, but they should offer few and little. Their role is to share our thoughts and feelings: they should be flexible about how we may want to use them.

Married, single or widowed? (delete as applicable)

> *We become very lop-sided individuals when we give up half of*
> *who we are. Good relationships require whole people.*
> Susan Jeffers, *Thoughts of Power and Love*, 1997

Someone who has lost a partner is *single*. The partnership is over; they are beginning a new phase in their adult lives. Many people will acknowledge this truism in public but will secretly have their own private fantasy that nothing has changed.

It's interesting to note that there is curiously no *formal* acknowledgement of the end of the partnership. Every other event in life has a ritual statement – birth, death and marriage certificates, educational qualifications, driving licences, divorce decrees – you even get a cycling proficiency certificate. There's the funeral of course but that is an occasion to mark the death.

We and those around us may be prepared to dwell on feelings about the loss of the person and our own grief but there is rarely a tangible or symbolic event or statement, which reflects on the partnership and declares it completed.

I'm not suggesting that there should be some event. However, because the closure of the relationship is *not* formally stated, the door is left open for fantasies and uncertainties to creep in.

People might admit shamefully to a close friend that, even years after the death, they still hold everyday conversations with their partner. As they're watching television they'll make a comment to be heard only by their partner's ghost.

Many people have talked about the pain – but eventual satisfaction – of finding some personal way of facing the finality of the relationship. One woman made a point of moving her wedding ring from her left to her right hand; someone else decided he would buy a new bed and reorganise the furniture.

At first, when asked your marital status you'll automatically reply 'married'; you'll become used to calling yourself 'widow'. You'll eventually know the strangeness – but freedom – of declaring yourself 'single'.

Peter would have wanted you to find someone else

> *How I longed for a nice kind man who would still accept me*
> *and even find me special and beautiful – and yet allow me my*
> *own sacred, hallowed past. I know I was asking the impossible*
> *in those painful early days. I felt like the wounded birds my*
> *children used to bring home who needed to be left in a*
> *cardboard box with cotton wool padding and fed and stroked*
> *from time to time until they healed.*
>
> Virginia Ironside, *You'll Get Over It!*, 1996

Our first thoughts in bereavement may well be 'How can I replace what I've lost?' It will be some time before we can face the surprising, but hard, truth – replacement is not an option and neither *should* it be.

Just because, at present, we can't imagine ourselves as 'single' doesn't mean that we should think, in the short or long term, about 'finding someone else'. Our last experience of life outside a long-term relationship may well have been in our youth when we were fuelled with personal growth and the impulse to create a family. Then was then; now is now.

It is likely that beneath our loss and grief we are now much more mature, resourceful and fulfilled in life than were our youthful selves; there may no longer be the same need to become 'bonded' in another relationship.

On the other hand some of us have defined ourselves in life by being part of a 'couple' and we want to resume this role as quickly as possible. There's no 'right' answer. There are strong advantages and disadvantages on both sides.

Advantages:

- an opportunity for a new, different life – an adventure
- a loving, sexual relationship
- the opportunity to make a 'wiser' choice
- company and support
- financial security.

Disadvantages:

- are we just trying to repeat the unrepeatable?
- can we risk not being found loveable?
- are we, yet again, giving up our independence?

- will we be making unfavourable comparisons with the incomparable?
- have we the energy and commitment to give to someone else – maybe even step-children?
- we may have feelings of disloyalty to our last partner.

Seeking another partner relationship

For I'm not so old and not so plain
And I'm quite prepared to marry again.

W. S. Gilbert (1836–1911)

The important thing is that we do what *we* want – as long as we are clear about *why* we want to do it.

At first we might never question a wish to resume a partnership with someone – it's what we've been happiest with all this time after all. What we don't always realise is that we'll have grown up a lot over the years. We'll have become (usually) more emotionally confident and self-assured.

We're likely to be without the doubts, insecurities and need for emotional support that may have lead us into intimate relationships in the past. The drive to settle down and have children may be absent.

We may have grown-up children and financial security. We may, rightly or wrongly, have put away our sexual needs. We may enjoy being independent. It's worth asking ourselves if we really want to get involved with someone else:

> *I have come a long way from those early days, from the years*
> *of putting myself through school again, to making those first*
> *tentative steps towards a career and financial independence. It*
> *had been a long-fought battle, and I was not willing to*
> *surrender my independence that easily. If I were to embark on*
> *a new partnership now, three decades later, it would quite*
> *simply have to be on my terms.*

Jeanette Kapferman, *When the Crying's Done*, 1992

We may think that because we are more confident and mature we have grown out of the embarrassment and awkwardness of adolescence – until we start 'looking for someone' in later life with a lifelong partner and grown-up family behind us. Young people are used to making new friends and becoming close very quickly: they are mostly attractive with an easily aroused sexuality. They can in general handle casual relationships and recover from disasters. Now, however, the prospect of an intimate partnership with someone else may well appear fraught with unexpected difficulties.

◆ If we've had a lifelong relationship we didn't notice so much how we both aged; even when in our sixties we may have felt just the same youthful and sexual people that we were at 21. Any new, other person will *definitely not* appear as though they were 21. We will have no knowledge of their younger selves and, at first, it may be difficult for both of us to establish the feelings of carefree abandon that we may remember from our youth. We are both more likely to be more 'serious' and 'realistic' about things; there may not be the same feeling of 'being swept off our feet' – which can be a disappointment.

◆ We, and our potential new partner, will almost certainly bring preconceptions and strong expectations about each other to our first meeting. If we've been in long-term relationships we won't be able to avoid comparisons with our previous partners and, at first sight, the new person won't measure up. It will take much longer than the first few meetings to see them differently.

◆ For many years we may have lived a very settled life – satisfying, comfortable, predictable and with not much happening. Our first experience of partnership all those years ago may have been one where we moved (with some relief) from a very hectic, socially active, unpredictable way of life into the quiet dependability of coupledom. It will seem unnatural and uncomfortable for us now to make the reverse journey from a previously fulfilled partnership into the uncertainty, embarrassment and discomfort of seeking a new relationship.

The sexual relationship we had with our dead partner may have been established as a youthful passion and may have grown and matured over the years – we may have been well-practised in knowing how to satisfy each other's sexual needs. It will have been particular and special to us.

Out of that relationship children may have been born. The continuation of sex after they left home may have continued to have reproductive associations. Both *new* partners' expectations of the other may be unmet and both may be disappointed that the other does not match up to their previous partner's sexual performance. There will need to be a commitment to re-learn much about each other's needs. On the other hand, we may be surprised at how much better sex is with a new person; this can bring its own guilt and regrets.

If sexuality is important to us we will see any problems as challenges. However, we may have fallen into a pattern with our dead partner which did not include sex or where it had been a problem. Now, the absence of sex may either figure strongly in our grief or it may even be a secret source of relief.

Most people who have been in long-term, worthwhile relationships, however, will have experienced much pleasure from sex. Frequently, indeed, sex will have improved in the latter years as the tensions and exhaustion of family life were reduced. Symbolically, physical intimacy will represent closeness – it can become physically and emotionally addictive.

When there is a sudden loss, our grief may focus on the withdrawal symptoms of sexual deprivation and an aching sexual neediness. This desperate physical yearning can feel dangerous. In our initial shocked state we can be tempted to seek some comfort in a brief liaison with someone else – anybody.

> *Because it had been so good I hadn't realised until she was in her last illness how much I could miss that part of our life together. It had been over a year since we'd made love when she died. I never let it show but as she became more ill, I felt so guilty that I was feeling more and more sexually frustrated and resentful.*
>
> *When she finally died I hated myself for feeling so obsessed about meeting someone else as soon as possible.*
>
> Robert Alwyn

For some people this might be a very satisfactory way of meeting their need for closeness, acknowledgement and sexual comfort: for most people, however, it won't be a good idea. Our associations of sex with 'specialness', loyalty, moral behaviour and happiness are usually so strong that we're likely

to come through it with feelings of regret and guilt to cope
with – never mind the 'surprised' attitude of other people.

'I'll never fall in love again...'

When we emerge from the first shock and despair of a
bereavement we may find ourselves alone and unsure about
our new identity. How we see the future will be strongly
influenced by our memories from adolescence when we were
about to make our way in the world.

People over 50 will think back to a time when social and
sexual rules were very different. There were very clear
guidelines for behaviour.

◆ We would have very polite social contacts, which would
  develop towards an eventual lifelong marriage.
◆ Sex was not recreational. It was acceptable only in the
  context of marriage. (It happened, of course, but furtively
  and in secret.)
◆ Men were dominant, women were modest; it was 'not done'
  for women to take a social or sexual initiative.

We may well have taken these attitudes into our marriages.
Divorce was shameful, adultery stopped just short of being a
crime. When we settled into a rewarding relationship we may
have set aside all these worries.

We will have grown with our dead partner into a private
intimacy with our own special, almost telepathic, way of
communicating – domestically, socially and sexually. Now,
stranded without our partner, we may be bewildered about
what to do.

◆ Many people will be influenced by strong widowist attitudes,
  which tell us that we should 'respect the memory of our
  partner' and come to terms with our 'aloneness'.
◆ We will be anxious about presenting ourselves as 'available'
  – we may simply not know how to do it.
◆ We may not be used to being in places where likely future
  partners are likely to be found.
◆ We know that social and sexual rules have changed since
  'our day' but we don't really know what they are (we'll have
  fears and fantasies, though).

Our most immediate concern may be about our appearance. We remember that 'in our day' making relationships was all about looking good. We were surprised how little this had come to matter in our relationship with our dead partner but the prospect of us looking for someone else with our bulges of fat and wrinkles seems faintly ridiculous. Surprising research, however, shows that we – particularly men – are generally much less interested in looks than people think. Being attractive may be important early on but when it comes to thinking about becoming partners we are much more interested in other factors – personality, warmth, sensitivity and sense of humour.

We associate romance with youthful bodies and assertive sexuality and as we become older we may imagine these concepts to be ridiculous when applied to us. Only 43 per cent of widows ever have a sexual relationship after they lose their partner (as opposed to 82 per cent of women who are divorced).

The truth is we may be prejudiced against ourselves. Actually, older people have an even greater skill and capacity for making new loving and sexually fulfilling relationships than young people. Look at our experience of life and the lessons we have learned about how to get along with people.

We may regret not being 17 – but remember the clumsiness and inexperience. Age brings assurance and an increased capacity for experiencing pleasure. For the first time we may feel free to take an initiative and ask for what we want sexually. Perhaps we should read some sex manuals and erotic literature. We may need to learn about safe-sex – maybe it didn't matter before.

The best rule of thumb is to trust our instincts: we should steer clear of anything that feels manipulative or coercive – if it feels good, it is good.

Paul Gebhard, a researcher, came up with a couple of interesting facts.

◆ If we've previously had pre-marital or extra-marital sex, we're much more likely to be motivated to seek a new partner than someone whose life has been only in a single relationship.

♦ A much higher percentage of widows than married women have orgasms in every act of love-making.

It may be a couple of years before we really gain an equilibrium, before we are sufficiently detached from the previous relationship to be able to present ourselves as an authentic individual – no longer a victim of loss. We need to re-create and 'love' ourselves before we are coherent and loveable to someone else.

> *And yet there may still be a yearning for companionship, hugs and sex which – early on – may be a straightforward need for physical and emotional support – not to be confused as the lead-in to a long relationship. Many people find this need satisfied by discreet no-strings casual affairs, which, if well conducted by people who know what they are doing, can bring some comfort. However, this time is also a time of vulnerability where intentions can be misinterpreted and feelings misread.*
>
> Virginia Ironside, *You'll Get Over It!*, 1996

How to find a new partner

Stop looking.

At least for the time being. There's no need to rush. Indeed it's been said that we need a year of readjustment for every four years of the partnership (which is surprisingly cruel advice to someone who was married for 40 years (rules are there to be broken).

Above all we must distrust any sense of urgency to *replace* our dead partner. Our interest in establishing a new relationship should be initiated by the *appeal of the other person* – rather than any generalised sense of restlessness in ourselves. It could be that there is a desperation to replace the emotional security from the previous relationship – or it may be that our dented self-esteem is telling us that we just can't manage on our own.

The first thing to do – and this is essential – is to get out more. You need to find the new 'you' in the context of other people. It will be hard at first but you should try, tentatively, to become part of one or more groups of people who share your interests. This is an opportunity to develop previously postponed activities, sports or hobbies. The idea is to place yourself amongst new people in new surroundings; it's only in these conditions that you will be able to re-create yourself as an unpartnered individual. It's best to find something to do which may be a totally new experience.

We should put out of our mind any thought of seeking or finding a new partner. Wait until we feel comfortable with our renewed social confidence.

Conclusion

Hello Anna, thank you for taking my call. My name's Jenny.
I'm ringing about my mother. She's 72 and has always been
very sprightly for her age. Well the problem is that my father
died six months ago – a heart attack. My mother's taken it
very badly – I can't believe how changed she is.

They were always very close – they'd have been married 50
years next May. She's always been such a warm, cheery
woman – always a friendly word for everybody and a shoulder
to cry on. Since my Dad died she's just gone completely to
pieces. She's depressed but won't go to the doctor's, she's let
her appearance go and I suspect she's started drinking in the
evenings. She refuses to open up about her feelings but on
Tuesday when I went round, I found her weeping. She said
'There's no point in going on any more now that he's gone'.
What was worrying was that she said that the only thing to
look forward to was when she 'could be with him again'. I'm
really worried about her, Anna, she's got a cupboard full of
pills and anything could happen.

Mind you, I can understand how she feels. It's very moving,
in a way, to see such love and devotion. Maybe it's true that
she won't find real peace until they're together again. I do
sympathise, but I'm so worried, Anna...

Caller, Talk Radio, 1999

There used to be a common Hindu practice – *suttee* – when a
widow would throw herself on her husband's funeral pyre.
Although in the West we find the idea repugnant, there is, here
and now, a living concept of 'emotional suttee'. Many people
will find – like Jenny – something to admire in her mother's
continuing absolute devotion. The idea that 'my life is
worthless without him' has a long-standing romantic pedigree.

We read with a tear in our eye about the elderly widower
who died six weeks after his wife 'of a broken heart'.

There may be an argument that such devotion is a sign of an enviable life-enhancing intimacy – that the sum of two lives is greater than their separate value. It's a comforting sentiment.

It would have some credibility if we did indeed give our *whole* lives to each other. Usually, however, we make use of our partners (in the nicest possible way).

◆ We look to them for emotional support and help.
◆ We use them as a mirror for our self-esteem.
◆ We look to them for physical comfort.
◆ We appreciate them for the things we can't do and the things we don't like doing.

This isn't selfishness because we're doing the same for our partner. However, the more – and longer – use we make of them for these purposes, the less need there is for us to have to think about these things ourselves and the more we will become disabled when our partner is no longer here.

It doesn't have to be like this. We should aim to support and complement each other but also to retain our personal 'wholeness'.

It doesn't mean we love them less; it means we love both of us more. And the more we love ourselves the more loveable we shall be.

Imagine the situation was different. What if *you* had died? What if you had left those you love disabled by distress?

◆ Would you be touched that their lives were so affected?
◆ Would you be flattered that your importance to them was so great that your loss had diminished their life?
◆ Would you be impressed that they had allowed their sense of themselves to have been consumed so entirely by our own needs?

Of course not. One of the main components of love and friendship is a respect for the wholeness and potential of the other person. We want them to make the most of themselves and live life to the full. We would expect them to be deeply saddened by our death but, after that, wouldn't we want to wish them well for the future?

We have a responsibility in our present bereavement for building on the good will of the lost relationship. At first we'll be helpless, but after a while we should accept that we have a responsibility – in honour of what we have lost – for our own re-growth. To remain lost in our grief, in a curious way, is a harsh judgement on the dead person – we're actually implying that their death is to blame for our helpless distress.

Most of this book has been about how we can lessen or repair the pain of bereavement, but there is more to the process for those people – and it can be all of us – who are able to work their way through the shock and distress.

Those who have known grief seldom seem sad.
Benjamin Disraeli (1904–81), *Endymion*

Successful grieving is not just about surviving loss caused by a death – it can be about becoming more grown up and in touch with life. Newly bereaved people may find such a positive outcome to be distasteful – even unacceptable – but, invariably, those people who can manage to come to an acceptance of the death will also report the changes for the better in their lives.

◆ We come to appreciate the importance of living in the present – savouring the here and now and relishing what we have here today, rather than harking back to past concerns or dreaming about hopes for the future.

◆ We learn to grasp opportunities spontaneously. We have learned that the moment will pass all too soon – and then we'll be sorry. We'll also have a greater awareness of using time more fruitfully, being more organised and resisting the temptation to put things off.

◆ We'll begin to start getting our priorities right. We'll remember how much time we wasted on trivial things now that we realise what the important things are.

◆ We'll realise the importance to us of other relationships. Losing someone is a hard way to realise the value of what we've lost but we'll become determined to appreciate friends and family in the future. If we've been well supported these relationships will have been strengthened and deepened.

◆ We'll have been 'forced' into a future where we have the opportunity to explore new potential in ourselves. We wouldn't, of course, have chosen it, but there should be no worry about making the best of it. We can be more curious and adventurous.

We've had a crash course in distress – we only *thought* we understood it before it happened to us. We're now able to empathise with other people in trouble. And not only bereaved people. Our emotions and coping abilities have been stretched and challenged. We know something now about pain, helplessness and depression, and this brings with it a humility, compassion and sense of responsibility, which will enable us to help others. We may not know what we will say to them, but we surely know what not to say.

We have learned – all of a sudden – what 'love' is. We never really knew before but now we are an expert.

> *Only people who are capable of loving strongly can also suffer great sorrow. But it is this very same ability to love which strengthens them and heals their grief.*
>
> Leo Tolstoy (1828–1910)

It all started with love and, in the end, it all finishes with love.

> *As long as I can I will look at this world for both of us. As long as I can I will laugh with the birds, I will sing with the flowers, I will pray to the stars, for both of us. As long as I can remember how many things on this earth were your joy. And I will live as well as you would want me to live. As long as I can.*
>
> Anon

Appendix I
Things to be Done

Within hours of the death – just when we are in a severe state of shock and confusion – we suddenly become the object of public interest and sympathy.

We'll be fortunate if we have close family members or friends who can handle this interest and allow us, for the moment, to be quietly on our own (if that is what we want).

◆ It's important that everyone who should know about the death is informed as soon as possible rather than learning from a third party. A phone call simply announcing the facts is all that is required at this stage with an assurance that they will be contacted again about funeral arrangements.

◆ Letters of condolence will begin to arrive, which should be promptly and briefly acknowledged.

◆ After a day or so when funeral arrangements have been determined people can be informed by letter – again there is no need to give personalised replies at this stage – that can be left to a later time. Something simple:

'Jane has asked me to write to you to thank you for your kind words of sympathy. She and the family would be pleased if you were able to attend the funeral at St Marks Church next Tuesday at 11 am, although they would understand if the short notice prevents this. Jane will write personally to you at a later date.'

We can also indicate any other immediate requests:

'No flowers please, but donations to ...'
'Family flowers only ...'
'No letters please ...'
'I would be pleased if you and Alan would join us here after the service for refreshments ...'

- We may wish to put a death announcement in the local paper:

  > ROBINSON – On May 9th at home, Christopher
  > Percival Robinson, dearly loved husband of
  > Catherine and father to Susan, aged 73 years.
  > Funeral service at Roundhill Crematorium,
  > Standerton on May 13th at 11am. No flowers
  > please: donation to Friends of St John's Hospice,
  > Holly Road, Standerton.

There will inevitably be a stream of offers – 'Do let me know if there's anything I can do'. This isn't just politeness. Most people, like us, are initially shocked, don't know how to respond and are very willing to become involved in some practical way. If we are inclined we can use their interest for their and our benefit. We may need someone who is thinking straighter than us to mobilise their support but there is much that may need to be done:

- cleaning
- cooking
- answering letters
- making phone calls
- looking after children
- taking the dog for a walk.

We will know who we want to be around us and whose presence will be unhelpful.

The funeral

Fortunately (or unfortunately), the shock of our loss often protects us from any anxiety about organising the funeral: we have more important things on our mind. A close friend or relative will – we hope – step in and kindly take responsibility. They will usually contact a funeral director.

At this time it may be important to have someone who knows all about caring for the body, registering the death, organising certificates and arranging a time and place for the funeral – someone to take charge in a world which has suddenly become chaos. There is nothing wrong with this. For most people there is much comfort from this outsider who can be strong, experienced, discreet and understanding.

Compared to other professional services, the funeral director's charges are mostly reasonable for the service and satisfaction provided. They are generally honest and reputable.

That is not to say that – even at this time of distress – we shouldn't be discerning. Someone should ask around before deciding which funeral director to use; nevertheless research has shown that nine out of ten people choose the first firm they approach.

In recent years a large proportion of the familiar long-established high-street undertakers have been taken over by a multinational – SCI (Service Corporation International) which has retained the firm's traditional appearance and staff but forced a 'hard-sell' policy on (unwilling) managers. There may be pressure to choose an expensive coffin, embalming, extra limousines and other costly services which an unwary customer may not realise they had agreed to. In other respects they will provide a satisfactory service but it is unfortunately necessary to realise that these firms are profit-driven – often run by regretful, old-fashioned 'professional' undertakers.

Burial or cremation?

We've all thought about what we want to happen to our body after we die. We usually don't dwell on it but many people nevertheless feel strongly about it.

Those who wish to be buried usually wish some part of their identity to continue – at least for some time.

People who opt for cremation are mainly drawn to the 'purification' effect of fire on decay.

If the choice was important to the person who has died, we, as their survivor, will almost certainly know their preference; if they never made it clear to us we can be assured that they were content to leave the decision to us.

If we are left with the decision, we should choose to do what we feel is most comfortable for us. However, the following may help with the decision.

Cremation

- There is an aspect of symbolic 'spiritual' 'cleansing' which some people feel appropriate.
- There is the undoubted hygienic advantage of dealing with the body's decay.
- Cremation is easier to arrange and costs half the price of burial.
- It is economical on land use.
- The final disposal is less stark and evident. There is a personal choice about disposing of the ashes.

However . . .
- The identity of the body is totally destroyed.
- The final resting place is not always easily identified.
- The process can seem mechanistic and impersonal.
- Emissions into the air are harmful to the environment.
- There can be no opportunity for exhumation.
- Crematoria are often less geographically accessible.

Burial

- The reality of the body's disposal is much clearer and more final.
- The location of the grave remains settled and memories can be more focused.
- The ceremony around burial is usually more personal.
- Burial is ecologically safer.
- The recycling of the body – 'dust to dust' – seems more 'natural'.
- Arrangements can be more flexible – home burial, woodland graves, burial at sea.

However . . .
- We may find it hard to think about the continuing decay of the body.
- The 'permanence' of the grave is illusory; most graves will be re-used within a hundred years.
- There are often more religious associations with burial – which may be unacceptable to some people.
- It may be difficult to organise a grave where you want it at

short notice.

♦ It will be very expensive and will need to be maintained in the future.

Embalming

One of the first questions a funeral director may ask will be 'Will you be wanting to view the body?'

Within a couple of days of death a body at room temperature will show signs of deterioration – discoloration and an odour of decay. This can make any viewing unpleasant.

You will be advised by a funeral director that they can provide 'hygienic treatment' – embalming. Sometimes it may be done as a matter of course (and with additional cost).

The fluid used in embalming – formaldehyde – is pumped through the circulatory system and injected into the abdomen. It's effective in arresting the development of decay and colouring in the fluid helps retain a 'warm', 'living' appearance. This may be comforting for people who wish to retain a memory of a loved one's appearance 'as they were in life'. The closer we were, however, the more we will have to acknowledge that the body's appearance bears no resemblance at all to the living person: no matter how successful the preservation, it will be very clear that the body is lifeless.

If the body remains at home and will be viewed during the time leading up to the funeral it is essential that it is embalmed or kept well chilled. This may be the case if other people travelling from a distance wish to pay their last respects before the disposal.

However, if as usually happens nowadays, the body is kept with the funeral director (where it can be viewed), they will have chilled storage facilities, which will prevent marked deterioration before the funeral.

Embalming is only effective in the short term: decay will resume as normal within a few weeks of burial.

There are concerns about the effect of formaldehyde, which is extremely toxic, on the environment – seeping eventually into the ground or being emitted into the atmosphere. This may or may not be an important factor – particularly at a time when our decisions are subjective and fired by emotions. You will know whether you want the body to be embalmed or not. Trust your judgement and make things clear to the funeral director from the outset.

If you are not satisfied with the service you get from a funeral director you can contact: either The National Association of Funeral Directors or The National Society of Allied and Independent Funeral Directors (SAIF) (see page 189).

Home organised funerals

In the immediate period following a death we are generally so preoccupied with the shock and distress of it all that we are usually grateful for a funeral director to come in and relieve us of all the arrangements for the funeral. They're the experts after all; there is even a feeling that it would be improper not to use their services. There is the added advantage that their familiarity with the process gives stability and reassurance at a time of confusion and stress.

There is much to be said, however, for the bereaved family and friends playing a much bigger part in the organising of the funeral. Imagine how much would be taken away from a family if, following an engagement, arrangements were simply handed over to a 'wedding director' to organise an off-the-peg wedding. Most people think that the details of the ceremony and the reception are most important; the intricate planning will take months. Most weddings will resemble each other superficially but all will be different – reflecting the needs and wishes of the participants.

Conventional funerals, however, are usually all alike. There will be some variation in the music and the address by the minister but mostly they are indistinguishable.

◆ They will usually be based on a religious model. This is appropriate if you consider the original purpose of a Christian funeral was to reflect on the piety of the dead person in their lifetime and to commend their soul to a successful spiritual afterlife. If this is *not* your intention, the religious ceremony may feel inappropriate.

◆ They will usually be impersonal. Rarely, the person who has died will be well known to a minister who will be able to talk with feeling and personal experience about the 'specialness' of the dead person's life. More commonly, however, the ceremony will be conducted by a 'duty minister' in a bare crematorium. The things that need to be said about the dead person are likely to remain unsaid.

◆ If it's a normal Western-Christian ceremony there will be pressure on the participants to 'behave well'. The traditional style of a church service does not encourage the open expression of emotion. If we want an atmosphere of joyous, expansive celebration of a life well-lived, we must create it ourselves.

Twenty years ago, if we wanted to organise a funeral ourselves people would have thought we were odd. If we are from an older generation we may shy away from the idea. However, we should be reassured that home-organised funerals are commonplace today. If you talk to crematorium staff and funeral directors they will all agree that the 'best' funerals are those where there has been a close involvement and participation of the family and friends.

And then there's the cost

It may not be a relevant factor but arranging a funeral ourselves is a much less expensive option. The national average cost of a funeral is about £2,050 when it includes a burial and over £1,215 when a cremation is involved. We may protest that there is something unseemly about looking for 'value for money' in a funeral. Most people, however, when it comes to their own funeral would prefer that the expense should not be extravagant.

It is possible (and easy) nowadays either to organise everything ourselves or use a funeral director flexibly – playing a much fuller role in the arrangements. We can choose how much we want to be involved and which services we wish to pay for.

We may find pressure from some High Street funeral directors to hand over all arrangements to them at unspecified – but much higher – prices. It is worth someone ringing around several firms to find reasonable prices – if only to put a marker down against growing exploitation within certain parts of the funeral 'industry'.

The first thing to be said to someone wishing to organise a funeral themselves is that, unless they are very resourceful and have willing assistance from family or friends, it is probably unwise to *begin* thinking about it only *after* the death has happened. There is much to be considered, the potential for embarrassing mistakes is great and you only have one chance to get it right.

However, the rewards for all concerned can be immense. *The Natural Death Handbook* (ed. Nicholas Albery, The Natural Death Centre, 1998) in spite of its forbidding title, is a mine of helpful information and addresses for people wanting to do-it-themselves.

Storing the body

The first task will be to wash and lay out the body. Anyone is capable of doing this – it means resting a pillow against the jaw to close the mouth, closing the eyelids and packing all the orifices with cotton wool. If you do not wish to do this a community nurse from your local health centre may be willing to do so.

If the death was at home you will need to decide whether you want to keep the body there or arrange for it to be kept in chilled conditions at a funeral director's, or – they like to be helpful – a hospital mortuary.

At home we will need to provide a cool environment – maybe supplemented with dry ice. If we want people to view the body and the funeral is not going to be for a week or so, we should think about embalming – it will be difficult otherwise to prevent odour and signs of decomposition.

Most people, however, will wish the body to be kept elsewhere. A funeral director may be willing to provide this single service for a few pounds a day.

Getting a coffin

Buying a coffin is not something we do every day. Some years ago it was almost impossible, but now there is a reasonably wide choice of suppliers and styles. We should be wary of some funeral directors who will willingly supply us with a £50.00 coffin for £350.00.

If we are environmentally minded a cardboard coffin may be an option. This is a well-constructed, sturdy container, which can be painted or covered with a pall. It can be bought in advance as a flat pack, which can be easily stored, or you can get one direct from the manufacturers Natural Burial Company/Eco-coffins (see page 190) – for about £140.00 which includes courier delivery.

The *Natural Death Handbook* will provide hundreds of local addresses, but the suppliers listed on page 190 are reputable and reasonable suppliers to be going on with. If you contact them they will send you full details of their product range.

Transport

Transporting the coffin to the cemetery or crematorium is one of the more difficult things to arrange. We make such a strong association of funerals with conventional hearses that any other form of transport seems inadequate and tasteless; a hired van seems too 'ordinary' and a large estate car seems overly casual. Many funeral directors are willing to provide a hearse and driver as a single service.

Booking a cremation or burial

We tend to be in awe of crematoria and cemeteries – mysterious places only to be approached through the medium of the funeral director. However, my experience of the management and staff is that they are very keen to deal directly with private individuals who wish to arrange something more unusual and personal.

Don't be nervous of stating your exact requirements – even better, ask for an appointment to visit to discuss the details: the procedure for the arrival, placing and removal of the coffin, music, seating arrangements, collection of ashes or preparation and filling in of the grave. You'll be surprised how keen crematorium staff are to be helpful.

Carrying the coffin

Traditionally coffins are carried by four or six bearers. This could be a problem:

◆ A coffin containing a body is very heavy indeed – so we'll need some strong people.
◆ Bearing a coffin on your shoulder is tricky; it requires muscles never used before and it's not the sort of thing that can bear much 'rehearsal'.

If the body has been kept in a mortuary or at a funeral director's they may be willing to lend you a trolley.

The funeral ceremony

Somehow, rooted in our unconscious, many of us have the idea that some sort of solemn, 'spiritual' ceremony is necessary; to do otherwise seems tasteless, to do nothing is faintly scandalous. And yet such occasions are usually dreaded.

Although ministers today try to make the ceremony as personal as possible, there is usually not the opportunity for them to brief themselves sufficiently and everything seems impersonal.

A good solution is to contact the British Humanist Association (BHA) (see page 188) who will put you in touch with a local 'officiant' (if there is one). He or she will contact the family or friends and find out enough about the deceased to conduct a personalised ceremony – usually at a crematorium.

There are about 170 officiants accredited to the BHA. They come from a variety of backgrounds but each is carefully selected and undergoes a process of training and mentoring. There are equal numbers of men and women and each will perform an average of 35 ceremonies a year. (They sometimes also officiate at weddings.)

The ceremony will be short – crematoria are usually booked for 30 minutes. There will be an emphasis on celebrating the life of the deceased, recalling their beliefs and regretting their loss. There may be short readings or music but the officiant will tailor the ceremony to the wishes of the family.

There will be a charge, usually paid through the funeral director. This will vary in different parts of the country but it should be similar to the fee charged by a minister for a funeral service (around £150 in 2005).

A second solution is for the family to do it themselves. Most people who have attended a home-planned ceremony will agree that it can be very moving and satisfying. There are, of course, opportunities for embarrassing silences and excessive sentimentality but, even so, the fact that it 'comes from the heart' makes up for any awkwardness.

There is a problem, though. Arranging a special ceremony, *more* than other aspects of a funeral, is complicated. It's not something that can be easily done in a couple of days and it will need someone with the strength and confidence to hold it all together.

However, there is help at hand in the form of a book – *Funerals Without God* (Jane Wynne Willson, British Humanist Association 1989) available from the BHA (£8.50 plus postage).

It's probably best if two or three friends or family members put together a recital of reminiscences, anecdotes, reflections, favourite readings and music. You don't need to say much but what you do say should be honest and positive. You could ask other participants if they want to make a personal contribution.

All chapels and crematoria have facilities for playing recorded music and this can be a powerful part of the ceremony.

There is a third alternative to a conventional funeral – not to have one at all.

Circumstances may be such that the prospect of the funeral – for whatever reason – is unbearable. There is no rule that there should be any ceremony. Maybe a couple of family members could accompany the coffin and be there silently when it is disposed of.

However we organise a funeral, we should remember that there is 'no rush'. Provided that the body is kept chilled, the funeral need not take place for several weeks. This can make a difference when it comes to planning a ceremony, acquiring a coffin, booking a venue or organising the attendance of far-flung family members.

However things are arranged, they should suit the needs of the bereaved survivors.

Home burials and cremations

Many people are drawn to the idea of a funeral on their home ground. This is perfectly legal but there are obvious problems.

◆ Public Health regulations demand that a grave should be 40 feet away from any water course – which rules out many homes (the mains water supply is a watercourse).

◆ You will need to know about the location of underground pipes and cables.

◆ How will the grave be dug – it needs great skill and heavy machinery; there are serious safety issues about the sides collapsing.

◆ You will need to know what will happen in the future should you wish to sell the house.

Woodland burials

This is the most economical, natural and environmentally friendly solution. There are now over 70 woodland burial sites in the UK. They are run by a variety of organisations – farmers, local authorities, wildlife charities, private trusts or individuals.

The grave is a peaceful rural setting. After the ground has settled a young tree will be planted. Eventually woodland will be created providing a habitat for birds and wildlife as well as providing a pleasant place to enjoy the countryside. A record of the burial site will be kept for people to locate the grave.

Woodland burial is in sharp contrast to the technology and pollution of a crematorium and the regimented solemnity of an urban cemetery.

There is an Association of Nature Reserve Burial Grounds, which is proposing a code of practice that emphasises:

◆ that the protection of wildlife should be a major consideration

◆ that shrouds, clothing etc. should be made of environmentally acceptable materials

◆ that people should be able to organise funerals by themselves if they wish

◆ that coffins and shrouds should be available to the public at a reasonable price.

Further details of woodland burial sites can be found in the

Natural Death Handbook or from: The Association of Nature Reserve Burial Grounds, at The Natural Death Centre (see page 189 for the contact address).

The funeral gathering

For someone who has been plunged into bereavement only a few days earlier, the funeral gathering is a time of sharply mixed feelings.

In many ways it seems such a cruel ordeal to inflict on people who only minutes earlier had seen the body being consigned to the cremator. Who could possibly expect someone who has just undergone the most traumatic week in their life to preside over such a social occasion? As participants, we have faced these occasions in the past with apprehension and uncertainty. Wouldn't it be better for all concerned if we attended the funeral and then just went our own separate ways?

If we feel strongly as the principal mourner that we really can't face such a public get-together, we should feel that we can stay away – everyone will understand. However, there is much to be said in defence of funeral gatherings. In many ways they can be the most important part of all the proceedings.

Until then the emphasis has been on celebrating and regretting the past and experiencing the personal pain of the present. The moment the body has been buried or cremated the focus shifts and the funeral gathering is where the change happens.

◆ The participants can acknowledge that the formalities have now been completed. The body is 'at rest' and it is now a question of 'picking up the pieces'.

◆ Memories of the dead person can be shared and their future 'remembered identity' can be defined.

◆ A funeral will have put pressure on estranged family members to come together; however much they don't get on with each other they're still 'family' – it's like an Extraordinary Annual General Meeting. The family can look around at each other: 'This is what we look like now. How shall we heal over the wound caused by our loss and how will it change us?'

◆ There will be chinks in the wall of tension and grief as

someone recalls a funny incident from the past (tentatively at first); relaxed laughter may be heard for the first time in a week.

◆ Friends of the deceased will begin to know whether they will have a continuing relationship with the family.

◆ As people get ready to leave there will be the first talk of the future; the fractured family has re-grouped, there has been some emergency social surgery and family strengths are re-affirmed.

On the other hand, such occasions are not without risk.

◆ The reasons people may have been estranged from each other in the past may easily become inflamed, and alcohol-fuelled resentments and accusations about the past may suddenly be let loose.

◆ Everyone will bring their own feelings of regret, blame, guilt and vulnerability about the death; put in the same room with others, the potential for recrimination and accusation is great.

◆ The positive aspects of looking to the future may be tarnished by greed. There is likely to be some curiosity about what will happen to the dead person's money and possessions. If such thoughts are put into words things may take an ugly turn.

For these reasons – and because the main mourner shouldn't be burdened with the responsibility – it's worth asking someone, who is not so directly affected by the death, to be 'in charge' – but staying in the background.

Traditionally these occasions are held in the family home. There's no rule that says this should be so – in fact there's much to be said for using a 'neutral' venue; we may not be happy about the state of the house, dozens of people crammed into a small space can be overwhelming and we can do without having to clear up the mess.

Gravestones, memorials and mementoes

It's important to many people that someone who has died should not only continue to live on in their memories, but that their death should be publicly marked in some material form. This may take many forms but a headstone on the grave is the preferred way.

Ordering a stone for a grave may be involved in the arrangements for the funeral but this is usually unwise. The filled grave should be allowed to settle before adding the stone and this may take several months.

It is also wise to allow some time to elapse to decide what exactly is wanted. There are likely to be a limited range of shapes, materials and sizes that are acceptable and available, so you should talk to your local stonemason who will know the particular requirements of local churches and cemeteries.

It is likely that cemetery and church authorities will also have clear opinions about the wording you can use – 'reverential and respectful,' rather than informal or whimsical.

You will have to pay over £460 for an average gravestone: and that's just for the stone. The more words (£4.60 a letter) the more expensive – like a very robust telegram. Getting permission to erect it and paying for the work to be done will add a further £200.

Crematoria have memorial walls in their grounds where stone plaques can be placed for a (renewable) period of years. You can also usually have a rose bush planted (depending on available space). This is likely to be expensive as it includes a charge for ground maintenance.

Sorting out the estate

The executor – named in the will – is in charge of dealing with the deceased's affairs. If no one was named, or there was no will made, someone will have to apply for letters of administration. This process puts someone in the same position as an executor – except that they will be called the administrator. (Administrators and executors will need application forms – look up 'Probate Registry (High Courts of Justice)' in the phone book for the local office.)

Whether executor or administrator, they are the personal representative of the person who has died. They are responsible for paying all the deceased's debts, taxes and expenses, including funeral expenses. They make the payments from the estate – not from their own income or savings. Only when these duties are finished can the personal representative share out the rest of the estate.

If you are a personal representative you may have to apply to prove the will: probate. This will give official confirmation of your power to deal with the estate and to pay the bills.

There are good reasons for probate:

◆ it looks after the interest of the deceased's creditors
◆ it protects the interests of any surviving dependants
◆ it checks that the estate will be distributed correctly.

Probate is not always necessary – it depends on the size of the estate. Normally, if the sums involved are small, organisations like the Post Office, banks or insurance companies are helpful and don't require the production of evidence of probate. However, if there are considerable sums involved, they will almost certainly wish to see the Grant of Probate or Letters of Administration.

The person who applies for a grant of probate should be over 18 and can be any one of the named executors. If there is a will but no named executor, they should be the main beneficiary.

If there's no will, it should be the next of kin, in this order:

◆ the surviving spouse
◆ a child of the deceased (or a grandchild if there are no living children)
◆ a parent of the deceased
◆ a brother or sister of the deceased
◆ another relative of the deceased.

It is not necessary to employ a solicitor, but you should be aware that the handling of complicated estates can become a very onerous and responsible business. It is at this stage when you become very grateful (or otherwise) for the orderliness of the dead person's affairs.

If the whole estate comes to less than £5,000 it may be possible for it to be released without proving the will or obtaining letters of administration.

Normally debts, including funeral expenses, are paid out of the deceased's estate. It's important that details of all money owed should be easily available – otherwise the personal representative will have to decide when everything has been claimed.

The personal representative should check out with the Inland Revenue, insurance companies, employers or others whether there are payments or refunds due. (Don't forget refunds of car tax and insurance.) As the executor or administrator, you can claim any arrears of Social Security benefits still owing to the deceased. There may be money due if the deceased was receiving or had recently claimed a benefit.

The application for a grant of probate

After all your enquiries and research you will be ready to complete the documentation which is put together and sent to the Probate Registry.

In due course you will be asked to meet with a probate officer to go through the paperwork and to sort out any problems: it should be fairly informal – not an 'investigation'.

Then the probate officer will let the personal representative know whether there is a tax liability – particularly for Inheritance Tax. You will also be asked to pay a probate fee (another testamentary expense). This will not come to more than a few hundred pounds for the largest estate.

The Grant of Probate or Letters of Administration will not be granted until any outstanding tax bill has been paid – you have six months to do this (in instalments or in full).

For a small fee you should get some copies of the document as they will be required before funds will be released.

Distribution of property

When all the expenses, debts and taxes have been paid, the personal representative may then distribute anything left of the estate according to the will or the intestacy rules. If there are no entitled blood relatives, the Crown has a right to the whole of the estate. You should write to: The Treasury Solicitor's Department (BV), Queen Anne's Chambers, 28 Broadway, London SW1H 9JS.

Whether someone is related or not, they can apply for a

share of the estate if they were being supported financially in any way by the person who died, immediately before the death.

Where a deceased partner has left money owing, you may need to check with an advice centre or a solicitor about any liability for the debt.

If you have any difficulty in dealing with the dead person's property, possessions or guardianship of their children, get advice from a solicitor or Citizens Advice Bureau as soon as possible. Get the leaflets 'Legal aid guide' and 'Getting legal help' from a Citizens Advice Bureau, public library, police station or a court, to find out if you can get legal aid. These places also hold a list of local solicitors which shows whether they take legal aid work and if they specialise in probate.

Disposing of personal possessions

When someone dies their *body* is disposed of; we shall never see them again. However, all around us remain potent memories: their possessions. Other people will reassure us that they are 'just things' – but we know that they are something more. Close association with the dead person will have given such objects a special identity. While they remain, powerful memories will persist. There are two temptations.

◆ Some people will find it unbearable to have such vivid reminders around. They will, in their first shock, want to bundle them up and get rid of them as quickly as possible.

◆ Others will want to cling on to these objects indefinitely; while they remain, something of the loved one remains alive.

Both of these responses are understandable – but dangerous. They both show our wish to deny our loss. It is unwise to get rid of things quickly – their existence can be comforting, preserve a sense of reality and soften the sharpness of the loss. On the other hand to preserve possessions indefinitely may feed the illusion that our lives have not been transformed.

Some things we shall want to keep forever but most people find it easiest to adjust the rate at which we get rid of the rest to match the pace of our own gradual adjustment to the death.

People to tell

This can be a tedious business. With luck we'll have someone to help us. Nevertheless there will be documents to send off.

◆ The deceased's passport to the Passport Office. You can get the address from the Post Office.

◆ Order books, payable orders, or girocheques to the Social Security office or other office which issued the payment. This applies also to a Child Benefit book that includes payment for a child who has died. Orders should not be cashed after the death of the person. It may be useful to keep a record of pension book numbers or other Social Security numbers before you send anything back.

◆ The deceased's driving licence to DVLA, Longview Road, Swansea 5A6 7JL.

◆ The registration document of a car, for the change of ownership to be recorded.

◆ Any season tickets. Claim any refund due.

◆ Membership cards of clubs and associations. Claim any refund due.

◆ Library books and tickets.

◆ Any National Insurance papers to the relevant office.

◆ Any equipment such as wheelchairs, hearing aids, artificial limbs should be returned.

We'll also need to inform:

◆ the offices of the local electricity, gas or telephone company

◆ the local social services department of the council if the person was getting meals-on-wheels, home help, or day-centre care or had an appliance or piece of equipment issued by the department

◆ any hospital the person was attending

◆ the family doctor to cancel any home nursing

◆ the Inland Revenue

◆ the Benefits Agency if money was being paid directly into a bank or building society account, for example Retirement Pension, Attendance Allowance

◆ any employer and trade union

◆ a child or young person's teacher; employer or college if a parent, brother, sister, grandparent or close friend has died

- the car insurance company (if you are insured to drive the car under the deceased's name, you will cease to be legally insured)
- the local council housing department if the person who has died was living in a council house
- the local council Housing Benefit/Council Tax Benefit section if the person who has died was getting Housing Benefit and/or Council Tax Benefit
- the Post Office so that they can redirect the mail.

We'll learn a lesson from all this time-consuming effort and searching around for addresses and telephone numbers. We can keep our own affairs in order and easily accessible as a gift to our survivors when our time comes.

Appendix II
Welfare Benefits following a Death

Help for the bereaved

If you are married and your husband or wife dies there are different kinds of payment you can receive depending on your age and the number of children you have living with you. Also, as of December 2005 financial aid for those widowed has been extended to include couples who have registered a civil partnership. The amount received is based on the deceased partner's level of National Insurance contributions.

Bereavement Payment

When your partner dies you may get a Bereavement Payment. This is a tax-free lump sum – currently, £2,000 – paid as soon as you are widowed, if your partner has paid enough National Insurance contributions and the recipient is under retirement age. (Pension age is 65 for a man, and 60 for a woman.) Bereavement Payments must be claimed within a year of death.

Widowed Parent's Allowance

You may be able to get Widowed Parent's Allowance if you are already claiming Child Benefit, or if you are expecting your partner's baby. The basic amount will depend on the deceased partner's National Insurance Contributions, but the standard rate presently stands at £79.60.

Bereavement Allowance

Bereavement Allowance is a weekly payment that can be claimed for up to 52 weeks from the death. The recipient must be over 45 years old, but not retired. You *cannot* receive

Bereavement Allowance at the same time as Widowed Parent's Allowance, but if your Widowed Parent's Allowance stops with in the 52 weeks – due to Child Benefit terminating – you can claim Bereavement Allowance for the remaining period.

Increased allowances

If either you or your spouse were getting Retirement Pension, Incapacity Benefit, Child Benefit or Industrial Injury Benefit when they died, you may be eligible for an increased rate.

Help for guardians of your children

If someone is entitled to Child Benefit for a child they take into their family they can also claim Guardian's Allowance.

Normally both parents of the child must be dead, but the allowance may sometimes be paid where only one has died and they were divorced or never married (or where the surviving parent is in prison or cannot be traced.) The person who takes in the child does not have to be the child's legal guardian to claim the allowance.

Funeral expenses

If you are receiving Income Support, Housing Benefit, Council Tax Benefit or Pension Credit you might be eligible for help with funeral expenses.

Extra Christmas aid

If you receive certain benefits you might qualify for some extra money at Christmas. This 'Christmas Bonus' is a tax-free sum of £10 made a few weeks before Christmas. There is no need to make a claim for this as you will receive it automatically.

Income Support

Income Support is a Social Security benefit for people aged 16 or over whose income is below a certain level. You may be able to claim it if you are not expected to sign on as a jobseeker and you are, for instance:

◆ incapable of work due to sickness or disability
◆ bringing up children on your own
◆ aged 60 or over
◆ looking after a person who has a disability or registered blind.

You cannot normally get Income Support if you are working for 16 hours or more a week or if you have a partner (spouse or someone you live with as if you are married to them) who works 24 or more hours a week.

You can get Income Support on top of other benefits or on top of earnings from part-time work. If you have over £3,000 in savings the benefit will be reduced proportionately.

Receiving Income Support is a passport to other benefits that could add value to your income.

You may have to pay tax on some Social Security benefits.

The Benefits Agency publish a very useful guide – *What to do after a Death in England and Wales* – which you can get free from any of their offices. It sets out all the details in a very readable and clear way.

Further help for the bereaved

If you are on a low income and you satisfy the qualifying conditions you may be able to claim means-tested benefits. Possible entitlements include Housing Benefit, Council Tax Benefit, Child Tax Credit, Working Tax Credit or Jobseeker's Allowance. For advice and information contact your Social Security office or your local Citizens Advice Bureau.

Or if your partner died as a result of serving in the armed forces you may be eligible for financial aid from the Veterans Society (see page 190 for details).

Appendix III
Useful Addresses

British Association for Counselling and Psychotherapy (BACP)
BACP House, 35–37 Albert Street, Rugby, Warwickshire CV21 2SG
Tel: 0870 443 5252

British Humanist Association
1 Gower Street, London WC1E 6HD
Tel: (020) 7079 3580

British Institute of Learning Disabilities
Campion House, Green Street, Kidderminster, Worcestershire DY10 1JL
Tel: (01562) 723010

Carers UK
Ruth Pitter House, 20/25 Glasshouse Yard, London EC1A 4JT
Tel: (020) 7490 8818

The Compassionate Friends
(Head Office), 53 North Street, Bedminster BS3 1EN
Helpline: 0845 123 2304 Admin: (0117) 966 5202

The Foundation for the Study of Infant Deaths
Artillery House, 11–19 Artillery Row, London SW1P 1RT
Helpline: 0870 787 0554 Admin: (020) 7233 2090

Cruse – Bereavement Care
Cruse House, 126 Sheen Road, Richmond, Surrey TW9 1UR
Tel: (020) 8939 9530 Bereavement line: 0870 167 1677

Gingerbread
1st Floor, 7 Sovereign Close, Sovereign Court, London G1W 3HW
Tel: (020) 7488 9300

Hospice Information
St Christophers Hospice, 51–59 Lawrie Park Road, Sydenham, London SE26 6DZ
Tel: 0870 903 3903

Institute of Family Therapy
24–32 Stephenson Way, London NW1 2HX
Tel: (020) 7391 9150

Jewish Bereavement Counselling Service
8–10 Forty Avenue, Wembley, Middlesex HA9 8JW
Tel: (020) 8385 1874

Lesbian and Gay Bereavement Project
c/o THT Counselling, 111–117 Lancaster Road, London W11 1QT
Helpline: (020) 7403 5969

Macmillan Cancer Relief
89 Albert Embankment, London SE1 7UQ
Tel: 0808 808 2020

Miscarriage Association
Clayton Hospital, Northgate, Wakefield WF1 3JF
Tel: (01924) 200 799

National AIDS Helpline
Tel: (0800) 567 123 (Freephone)

National Association of Funeral Directors
618 Warwick Road, Solihull, West Midlands B91 1AA
Tel: (0121) 711 1343

The National Society of Allied and Independent Funeral Directors (SAIF)
SAIF Business Centre, 3 Bullfields, Sawbridgeworth, Hertfordshire CM21 9DB
Tel: 0845 230 6777

One Parent Families
255 Kentish Town Road, London NW5 2LX
Tel: (020) 7428 5400

Natural Death Centre
6 Blackstock Mews, Blackstock Road, London N4 2BT
Tel: 0871 288 2098

SANDS (Stillbirth and Neonatal Death Society)
28 Portland Place, London W1B 1LY
Helpline Tel: (020) 7436 5881 Office Tel: (020) 7436 7940

Terence Higgins Trust
52–54 Grays Inn Road, London WC1X 8JU
Tel: 0845 1221 200

The UK Council for Psychotherapy
2nd Floor, Edward House, Wakley Street, London EC1V 7LT
Tel: 0870 167 2131

Veterans Agency
Norcross, Blackpool FY5 3WP
Helpline: 0800 169 22 77. Minicom: 0800 168 34 58

Suppliers of coffins

Carlisle Bereavement Service, Cemetery Office
Richardson Street, Carlisle CA2 6AL
Tel: (01228) 625 310 Fax: (01228) 625 313

Heaven on Earth
18 Upper Maudlin Street, Bristol BS2 8DJ
Tel: (0117) 926 4999

Green Undertakings
12a Swain Street, Watchet, Somerset TA23 0AB
Tel: (01984) 632 285

Natural Burial Company/Environ Eco-Coffins
c/o Enrivon, Parkfield, Western Park, Hinckley Road, Leicester LE3 6HX
Tel/Fax: (01162) 333566

Appendix IV
Grief on the Internet

Death, dying and grief resources; these are large Web sites, which will provide links to most other sites of interest.

Hospice organisations in the UK and Ireland

http://www.hauraki.co.uk/hospice_uk
An up-to-date list of hospice information pages on the Internet

Bacup
http://www.cancerbacup.org.uk/home
Support for people with cancer and their families and friends.

Cancerlink
http://www.personal.u-net/com/-njh/cancer.html
Cancerlink is a resource service for cancer patients, family and carers.

Citizens Advice Bureau
http://www.citizensadvice.org.uk
This user-friendly site offers legal and financial information, and can direct you to your local office for free and independent advice.

GriefNet
http://griefnet.org/
This award-winning Web site is your international gateway to resources for life-threatening illness and end of life care.

The Desktop Lawyer
http://www.desktoplawyer.freeserve.net/law/
Legal Information: Wills: Living Wills. You can download sample pro formas for doing it yourself.

Widow Net
http://www.widownet.org/
This is a resource for widows and widowers, and is based in the USA. The book list is good, particularly as it includes suggestions for reading from those who have been bereaved.

London Association of Bereavement Services
http://www.bereavement.org.uk
LABS has a good list of links to resources for the bereaved. Particularly noteworthy is its list of sites for people of different cultural backgrounds and religions.

SIDS (Sudden Infant Death Syndrome) Network
http://sids-network.org/
Many more children die of SIDS in a year than all who die of cancer, heart disease, pneumonia, child abuse, AIDS, cystic fibrosis and muscular dystrophy combined.

Kearl's Guide to the Sociology of Death
http://www.trinity.edu/~mkearl/death.html
Unlike many of the more psychologically-oriented pages in cyberspace, the orientation here is sociological. It is assumed that individual's fears of death and experiences of dying and grief are not innate but rather are shaped by social environments.

Natural Death Centre
http://www.naturaldeath.org.uk/
A fascinating Web site which looks at death impassionately. It is particularly strong on resources for alternative funerals. There is a link which gives access to the complete text of the 1994 edition of the *Natural Death Handbook*. A must.

Worldwide Cemetery
www.cemetery.org/
Monuments in the World Wide Cemetery allow people to share the lives of their loved ones in ways that traditional printed death announcements or stone inscriptions cannot.

The Death Clock
www.deathclock.com
You can find out your deathday (as well as other matters of interest).

Beyond Indigo
http://www.beyondindigo.com/
This site is very user-friendly and provides various resources to help those who have been touched by death.

The Compassionate Friends
http://www.compassionatefriends.org/
The Compassionate Friends is a national non-profit, self-help support organisation which offers friendship, understanding and support to bereaved parents, siblings and grandparents.

Dying with Dignity
http://www.dyingwithdignity.ca
Dying With Dignity is a registered charitable society whose mission it is to improve the quality of dying for all Canadians in accordance with their own wishes, values and beliefs.

Growth House
http://www.growthhouse.org/
Links to hospice and home care, bereavement, death with dignity, AIDS, and related topics in life-threatening illness make up the bulk of this site.

Safe Crossings
http://www.providence.org/safecrossings/
Safe Crossings is an anticipatory grief and bereavement programme supported by Hospice of Seattle.

The Kids' Place
http://www.kidsplace.org/
This site is an organisation dedicated to the task of providing a supportive environment to grieving children and their adult family members.

GROWW, Inc.
http://www.groww.com/
Grief Recovery Online founded by Widows and Widowers (GROWW) offers 100 pages of helpful information, links and resources on the path to healing.

Motherloss
http://www.freewebs.com/motherloss/main.html
This group was started to help with the grieving issues for adult children of Mums who have died. The site provides a place for individuals to share their stories.

Pen Parents
http://www.penparents.org
A support network for bereaved parents. The site helps in matching bereaved parents by the types of losses they have had or other special circumstances (i.e. single parents), so they can write to each other for mutual support and encouragement.

Pet Loss Grief Support Page
http://www.petloss.com
A guide to various aspects of pet loss bereavement, including articles on how to cope with the loss of a pet, poems, a book reference (and how to order), and a listing of links to other pet loss resources.

Twinless Twins
http://www.twinlesstwins.org/
A support for twins (all multiple births) who suffer from the loss of companionship of their twin through death, estrangement or in-utero loss.

Living Beyond Loss
http://adrr.com/living/
A personal account of living through the death of children, the grief process and what it means to survive. Essays and links provided.

Journey of Hearts
http://www.journeyofhearts.org/jofh
This Web site is for anyone who has ever experienced a loss or a significant life event that changed their life forever.

The Grief Recovery Institute
http://www.grief-recovery.com/
Internationally recognised in the areas of death education and people's reaction to loss. The Institute provides programmes for universities, colleges, health care professionals, care givers, and many others.

Appendix V
Further Reading

I Don't Know What to Say, Dr Robert Buckman, Papermac 1990

Merely Mortal, Sarah Boston and Rachael Trezise, Methuen 1988

The Human Animal, Desmond Morris, BBC 1994

The Which? Guide to Giving and Inheriting, Lowe, 1994

What to do after a Death in England and Wales, Benefits Agency Communications

Funerals Without God, Jane Wynne Willson, British Humanist Association 1989

Green Burial, J. B. Bradfield, Natural Death Centre 1994

Good Grief, Carol Lee, Fourth Estate 1994

A Grief Observed, C. S. Lewis, Faber & Faber 1996

What To Do After A Death, DSS Leaflets Unit, PO Box 21, Stanmore, Middx HA7 1AY

What To Do When Someone Dies, Which? Books, Consumers' Association 1991

Wills and Probate, Which? Books 1995

The Natural Death Handbook, ed. Nicholas Albery, The Natural Death Centre 1998

Concise Guide to Customs of Minority Ethnic Religions, David Collins, Arena 1993

Surviving Grief and Learning to Live Again, Wiley 1992

The Complete Guide to Reducing Stress, Chrissie Wildwood, Piatkus 1997

Green Burial: The D-I-Y Guide to Law and Practice, J. B. Bradfield, Natural Death Centre 1994

Loss and Bereavement in Childbearing, Rosemary Mander, Blackwell 1994

The Tasks of Grieving, Dr Tony Lake, Sheldon Press 1998

Good Grief, Barbara Ward and Associates, Jessica Kingsley Publishing 1993

Living with Grief, Tony Lake, Sheldon Press 1984

You'll Get Over It!, Virginia Ironside, Hamish Hamilton 1996

When the Crying's Done, Jeanette Kupferman, Robson Books 1992

The Handbook of Grief, eds Strobe and Hanson, Cambridge University Press 1993

The Initials in the Heart, Lawrence Whistler, Weidenfeld & Nicholson 1987

Self Esteem, M. Kay and P. Fleming, New Harbinger Publications 1987

Grief: Rebuilding Your Life after a Bereavement, Dr R. M. Youngdon, David & Charles 1989

Thoughts of Power and Love, Susan Jeffers, Coronet 1997

Secret Flowers, Mary Jones, The Women's Press 1988

Index